Lece,

I want I
have this hard back I
version of Elaine's remarkable
True-life story? –

Love,
Renie

Sharon
Leland

The King's Kid

Lost and Found

The Reborn Kid of the King

(The original, complete, untouched and updated
true life story of Elaine Elizabeth "Liz" Presley)

By

Irene Leland

(Compiled and presented by the author, based on the authentic facts,
as told to her by Elaine "Liz" Presley)

ISBN (Paperback): 978-1-7365062-2-6
ISBN (Hardcover): 978-1-7365062-5-7

Foreword

As the author of "The King's Kid", I am sincerely and immensely grateful to Elaine Presley for giving me the privilege of writing this biography. What a profound and meaningful experience it has been for me to feel as though I have been reliving her extraordinary life right along with her. Every step of the way, I am perpetually captivated by the deep, diverse and multifaceted magnitude of her journey in existence, from every angle, from all of the highs to all of the lows, from every hardship and obstacle to every celebration and discovery!

But much more than that, I have been impressed beyond any measure by Elaine's remarkable and steadfast ability to courageously forge ahead and climb over each and every hurdle, no matter how daunting…and to never lose touch with the strong sense of love within her, that she so endlessly gives to others.

This is the power of the human spirit. This is Elaine Elizabeth Presley. This is what builds her character more and more and what gives her the strength and vision to pursue!...And, in seeking, she finds! And, through her perseverance, she renews…over and over again.

I also want to note that Elaine's pleasing, positive attitude, her gravitating charm and her delicious, spontaneous sense of humor are magnetic qualities that naturally endear her to people.

And, to top it all off, she just happens to be the daughter of Elvis Presley. She is indeed "The King's Kid", kid of the king!

I am honored to share Elaine's astounding true saga. I am blessed to be her good friend. I have had the distinct pleasure of knowing Elaine for almost nine years and living with her for over five years. It has been a treasured joy for me to be part of her life! I am wishing her all of the best in the next chapters of all that lies ahead for her!

--- Irene Leland

Table of Contents

INTRO

Truth Awakens

Notation: Some of the names in the book have been changed for protection of identity purposes.

INTRO

Truth Awakens

On May 6th, 2013, a momentous consequence impacted the life of Elaine Elizabeth Boden and changed its course dramatically. Her earth shook happily, and her moon danced across the skies as a huge revelation burst into realization.

Sitting in her home in Wales, England on a chilly, rainy afternoon, it was as if the sun's brightest rays and most soothing warmth had just enveloped her. In superlative joy, Elaine jumped off of her sofa and proclaimed to the world in the room, as her dog, Quaver watched surprisingly, "Oh, my God, I'm Elvis Presley's daughter!"

At this important moment in time, looking backwards and forwards, the world surrounding Elaine suddenly came together in a magnificent and synchronized truth. It had always been about finding her real home, by searching and realizing who she really was and what it was all really about.

And, truly it had been a long, long journey for this special child, marked by determination, strength and unfathomable courage in dealing with "the unknown" in the midst of confusion, desolation and turmoil, to survive and to discover her own real identity and in doing so, to finally come home.

The overpowering, yet deeply gentle essence of Elvis in reality and spirit had been swirling around Elaine's entire existence since birth. And now all of these intertwining salient elements, both driving and subtle, had merged together bringing the remarkable and soothing awakening.

An Unusual Beginning

Let's turn the clock back in time to a very significant day in the year, 1959. On December 11th, David Mower made his unparalleled entrance into the world. He was born in Little Clacton On Sea in Essex, England, presumably the child of Mildred Hynard and Dennis Mower. David entered into a staunch army family. His "dad", Dennis was army active, having served a good while in Germany, and his mom had been in the army volunteer work for the Red Cross. A vast amount of mothers that gave birth there at Little Clacton On Sea Hospital came over from the German barracks, from English and American troops, as they wanted their babies to be English born. Mildred was simply coming home.

David proved from the very start that he was not an ordinary baby. It became evident that this little boy was quite a rare creation. He also was a girl. Although, on the obvious outside, he appeared to be a male, it did not take long to medically ascertain that he had female components...what became the beginning of a childhood discovery that would play out dramatically as his/her early life showed more and more of the natural little girl... physically, mentally and emotionally!...and in time, Elaine would emerge...

Baby David came home to a tiny shack in Marks Tey, not far from the town of Colchester. (Colchester is the hub of the Army barracks in England, to and from Germany and the world.) It was indeed an extremely primitive environment and way of living....no electricity and no plumbing. His mum, Mildred bathed him in an old English metal tub, with water from the well that she boiled. He was wrapped in "nappies" as diapers. After clothing was hand washed, it was strung and wrung out on a mangel to pre-dry before hung on the line. With no bathroom, David eventually learned to relieve himself in an outhouse about twenty yards away from the abode. At night time, in the pitch of the freezing dark, Elaine remembers uncomfortably, as David, walking blindly and very slowly to the site and inevitably tripping on an old rake which propelled upwards, hitting and bruising his head, and then later stumbling back to his bed.

A very strong and handsome young one...David was adored by his mother and also treated adoringly by his comrades. The girls especially loved being around him, as he was not like most of the boys! He had a real, sensitive and empathetic attitude, not to mention his humorous and fun loving antics, and as he grew older, his female peers gravitated to that warm instinct. They enjoyed his companionship and treasured the fact that David had an inclination to listen well and to be kind and understanding.

But going through the building blocks of life early on was not exactly a normal or comfortable process for David, due to several factors:

Firstly, living in a very modest home with very few resources certainly made for not an easy time.

Secondly, David's two siblings, James and Dora lived there as well, and it was a difficult relationship, as it became more and more obvious that he had very little in common with them. They treated David coldly and lived in their own separate "world".

Thirdly, Dennis was a fiercely firm "father figure". He put a lot of pressure on David to do many hard jobs and tasks inside and outside of the little house.

But, lastly and most dominantly, Dennis was dogheaded and determined to bring out the "man" in David. He hated the innate dual gender element in David, and this later played out to be a most unpleasant situation…

No doubt, it was a struggle living in poverty and total simplicity, not to mention dealing with the strained family relationship with Dennis' hard hand and the stark division between David and brother, James and sister, Dora. But David's mother was always there to comfort him and stand by him. Her steadfast devotion to him was always evident, from the very beginning. She never failed to rock him soothingly as a baby and to always tuck him safely in bed at night after reading him sweet bedtime stories.

Moving On Up

When David was about five years old, the Mowers moved to another home next to farm land, which was in the village of Coggeshall, a little over nine miles away from Colchester. It was believed at the time by David that the farm owners built the house for their dwelling, and it was exciting for David to watch this new custom made home come to life before they moved in!...a real livable three bedroom house!...with proper heating and water conditions to boot!!!...on the outskirts of the beautiful village of Coggeshall. It was assumed that the family was able to live there in exchange for Dennis working on the farm. He farmed during the week and logged on weekends.

Young David became accustomed to picking up the bails of hay on the farm and loading them on to the trailer behind the tractor. He also spent much time chopping and bagging wood in the woods about 2 miles away along with brother, James. (James had the duty of sawing the wood into big slabs that David would chop into smaller chunks. David was not allowed to do the big sawing or drive a tractor because of his delicate medical condition.) The wood pieces were then loaded into fertilizer bags and placed on the trailer and delivered to designated homes. James received pay from Dennis for these jobs, but David very rarely did.

Nevertheless, eager David always looked forward to pea picking and potato picking on other properties that had signs offering pay during the seasonal times of year. He would put the potatoes in large brown sacks. As for the peas, they were placed in metal buckets before being poured into meshed sacks. He also enjoyed picking through the black currants and tediously arranging them in compartments on trays. It was ultimately satisfying for him to bring his "goodies" to the stations for weighing and to; collect his monetary rewards.

As for other money makers, David sometimes caught eels in the river around Coggeshall and sold them to the local hotel in town. He also periodically washed cars and was proud to have his own paper route!

For fun, David found pleasure in picking wild strawberries, raspberries, gooseberries and blackberries in the fields. He happily brought his findings home to his mum, who would turn them into pies and crumbles.

In light of David's schooling life, he first attended St. Peter's Primary School. Then he moved on to Honeywood High School and eventually Alec Hunter High School for less then a year.

In school days, he was a very quiet child and quite shy. Sometimes, he was bullied and picked on due to his sensitive nature, and the kids used to call him "Flea Bags" because of his cheaper clothing. In contrast and on a lighter note, every so often, David would break out into his spontaneous comedic antics and inevitably "crack up" his classmates. Nevertheless, he had only a couple of friends. But, as previously noted, the girls naturally gravitated to him, as he had an uncanny way of understanding, sympathizing and bringing comfort.

Sometimes, David had trouble paying for his school lunches, and he often used to rummage for lunch tickets that had not been used. This was due to the sad fact that his mother was in slow decline and spending household money on alcohol. But when she did make him lunches, it was banana sandwiches, peanut butter with grape or strawberry jam sandwiches, butter and sugar sandwiches, cheese and pickle sandwiches or cucumber and tomato sandwiches.

Walking to and from school was a regular routine for David. But, on one unlucky day while walking to St. Peter's School, David was hit by a white van as he was crossing the street. This accident catapulted him to the side of the road, rendering him unconscious. Upon awakening, David was unable to walk. The driver carried him to David's house. It took three weeks for David to thankfully walk again. In aftermath, the driver often visited David and brought gifts.

In the midst of continual hard times with Dennis' overbearing demeanor, Mildred worked hard physically and emotionally to try and keep things together, but she was constantly confronted with Dennis' negativity. It was devastating enough for her to deal with his unfair treatment towards her, but what mostly hurt her was his stiff, demeaning attitude toward David. And, what was even more stingingly detrimental was the fact that Dennis never gave David any normal attention at all…as he knew down deep that David was not his child!

Nevertheless, Mildred never failed to give David her superior vigilance, as well as her very best in taking care of James and Dora. Elaine vividly remembers her/his mum taking him on jaunts to do grocery shopping in the town of Colchester, 9.6 miles away. It was always an adventure! Sometimes they walked about a mile to the bus. Sometimes Mildred rode the pushbike with David in the basket. Every now and then, she would make a stop at the pub, while watching over him, for a drink or two. David noticed that his pretty mum easily attracted the fellows who were looking on.

A Downward Spiral

Dennis maintained a bad track record as a hard bearing husband, an insensitive, mean father and a deceitful man:

He was continually yelling at Mildred and the kids about anything and everything! In one tiny illustration of that, Mildred sometimes dressed David in girl's clothes, knowing innately that he had an inclination and liking for that. Whenever Dennis found out, he would come down hard to stop it!

In example of Dennis' basic bad influence, while working with David on the farm nearby, he would occasionally go into the farm owner's shed and take away/steal certain tools. Later, when the thefts were recognized and reported, Dennis put the blame on David.

Most prevalently and unhappily, David felt constant pressure from Dennis relating to the issue that he was not a "full blown" boy. Dennis never let up on his driving force to turn his "son" into a football player and eventually an army guy! And, as previously stated, Dennis' obsession to bring out the "male" in David became a formidable actuality. He coerced him into having a crucial surgery, at the age of about five, to correct/enhance his masculine genitals. He scared David into it by telling him the story that if he didn't have the surgery then, the doctors said that waiting to perform it later could cause him cancer.

(These medical procedures were free, as paid for by the English government.)

This impending ordeal, adding physical stress to mental and emotional torment, was especially gruesome for burgeoning David, as he always felt down deep inside that he was really, truly a girl!

The delicate, serious surgery proved to be challenging, and in result of David spending three months healing in the hospital afterwards, it was decided that there needed to be adjustments made. Thus, while still in the critical children's ward, David succumbed to another surgery, which followed with more weeks of rehabilitation. Recovery on both counts was horrendous. Elaine lucidly remembers in aching anguish how tortuous and distressing it was for her/his little volatile body to get in and out of the Epsom salt bath, not to mention the agitating experience of the itching and the pain while in the bath!

As a pitiful result from these operative events that were not at all advanced and subsequently generating sudden testosterone levels, David became quite hyper, and he underwent periodic episodes of nervous shaking, confusion and unhappiness.

Unbelievably and sadly, Mildred had an undying love for Dennis, even throughout his abusiveness as a husband and a father. Her mother, known as "Nan" to David, was devastated that her daughter did not take many opportunities to leave him, but she could never take the giant step to break away. Mildred was strikingly beautiful, and any time another man would take a favorable look at her, Dennis would go "mad".

Interestingly, in light of all of this, with the broad sensibility of uneasiness, even along with provoking occurrences, Elaine explains that in retrospect, there was a general feeling of normalcy. (Of course, at the time, this was the only life that David knew.) She shares that David's "dad" never physically abused anybody, but he was known to shout out a great deal, grimly and vehemently! And, at Christmastime, he always treated the kids equally with presents, yet he never provided gifts on birthdays.

Overall, things were not terribly horrible, and Elaine within all of this, states that she was a simple, happy child. But as the future played out its developing role, the contravening aspects of Dennis' dominance generated disturbing and downcast results for both Mildred and David…The issues of Dennis' poor behavior laid out thus far paled in comparison to what later lay ahead…

Sequentially, David's mum sunk into a progressive decline. The deteriorating way of life with Dennis took a burdensome toll on her. It became clear that her emotional as well as mental capacity was becoming less and less stable. Nervousness set in which led to upsetting reverted characteristics, including the recurring motion of flinching her arms, turning and re-turning on devices and incessant chatter. Yet aside from these reactionary symptoms, it was also noticeable that there was something underlying, in and of itself that was off track with her state of mind. Repeated efforts to take her to the hospital for evaluation failed over and over. She defiantly resisted!

Mildred started on a growing pattern of finding relief through alcohol use, as well as prescription drugs. She never drank at home, but she had the habit of venturing to the pubs. Whether walking to the village of Coggeshall or catching the bus to the town of Colchester, she found refuge and temporary solace in the local drinking spots. Elaine remembers, as David, coming home from school to find his mum in an altered status. She never appeared obviously drunk, as she was able to function as best as she could, but he knew that this was not his normal sober mother.

Morosely, Mildred's poor condition and addictive reliance only mounted. It got to a very sad point when sometimes David, hanging out with friends in town, lamented over seeing his mum dejectedly sitting on a bench in the village across from the big clock. She would usually be in an off kilter nature, rapidly blinking her eyes and twitching her arm, while talking to herself. Her son naturally ran over to her side and tried to coax her to come with him…to no avail. But she reached out to hold him next to her on the bench…

Looking back on this ultimate reality, Elaine now ponders in full spectrum, and she is staggered over the stark contrast between the mum that David knew "before" with the mum that she had become. She vividly remembers the original, natural mother…so lovely and so sophisticated…so composed and in control…so unlike the later person that desperately grappled with the crippling situation that devoured her existence.

Clowning Around Town

Oh, did David ever have fun, fun, fun creating all kinds of innocent mischief with his pals in the village of Coggeshall! These happy go lucky episodes became a way of life and liberation for David between the ages of six and thirteen. The leader of the little gang was, of course, David, and he was joined by his buddies, Wayne and Paul. They were always brave soldiers, showing off their strength and conceptions! There were many crazy escapades which evolved into more and more wild pleasure!

One of the first silly achievements was the capture of the gnomes! This event was carried off at night time along the row houses that were neatly lined up on Tey Road. Each tiny house was like a duplicate of the next, and they each were contained in their own fenced in "box" with a gate at the front. One unlucky home owner had a multiple array of miniature concrete gnomes in her front garden. She had one gnome after another, living their own "gnome lives". Some were fishing in a little bird bath, some were lying down in rest, and others were sitting in chairs petting their cats. There were happy gnomes, laughing and clapping, and there were sad ones, looking down.

David and his crew set out on their gnome abduction to carefully seize these decorative dwarfs…but the playful warriors had no intention of stealing them!...Nor did they even wish to kidnap them for ransom! Oh no, they simply moved them from one front yard to another! David's concocted idea was to carry the gnomes over the low barrier between the houses and place them in the exact same spots, respectively, but in the next door neighbor's yard! Success! The little gnomes now had a new home!..Well, they hardly had a chance to get into their relocated routine, as the original owner had them brought back the very next day.

What a riot! The boys pulled it off, and nobody had a clue as to who the fugitives were! So, about a month later, the runaway daredevils decided to do a re-run! Yup! Same action in the same place! But, this time…oh dear, they got caught! The gnome owners yelled out at them in the act and chased them as they ran down the street. They could tell who they were, as the boys lived not too far away on 42 Tey Road. There was a mild confrontation that followed which resulted in a slap on the ear!

Moving on to the realm of plights at night, but in a more modest mode, David, Paul and Wayne got a huge bang out of running through the church grounds when it was dark! Many times they would run, with sheets tucked in their arms, to the graveyard site. Hiding behind the big gravestones, they would cover themselves in the sheets and then pop out from their posts, flagrantly jumping around as dancing ghosts and vocally spewing out the "Wooooooohhhhhh"!!!!!!! To get alarming and scared reactions from passers-by was a chill and a thrill!!!

Now, to make a point clear, in all of these antics and pranks, there was never a mission to hurt or "get back" at anybody…it was a natural and crazy fun adventure in letting go and testing the field as well as each other!

One really humorous and ridiculous endeavor happened on the flat roof of a co-op in town. One of the team was on the roof holding a cup of water. The other was on the sidewalk below. As a walker walked by, the accomplice on the ground level, in careful cue with cohort above, asked the person walking by, "What's the weather report?" The walker said, "Oh, looks like sunny to me!" With that, the "roof bird" replied, "Well, it's raining now!" and then he unleashed the water down on his head! Eventually, the antique shop owner next door, spotting them in the front of his store, came out and dumped a bucket of water on the guys, saying, "Now, it's really raining!"

At the end of Tey Road, into the village, there was a large circular area of Coggeshall with residences all around. A favorite escapade for the boys was to play like marines and run around the circle in the back of the buildings from one house to the other, sometimes jumping over fences and barricades. One house proved to be a particular challenge as it was a big mansion with high walls, and the home owners had a big black dog that definitely did not like intruders! David and his fellow "marines" took this provocation seriously and daringly! They climbed over and down that wall, charging in stead and across the back property, alerting the furious dog to go after them! The stimulation was to arrive at the other end of the formidable wall and climb up and away without being "destroyed" by the canine! No destruction, thank heaven!

A perfect yearly forum for David's capers was the holiday, Guy Fawkes Day and/or Guy Fawkes Night. It was the annual Bonfire Night held mostly in Britain on November 5th. (similar to the July 4th firecracker festivities in the USA.) This event celebrates the survival of King James 1 in 1605 when Guy Fawkes, a member of the Gunpowder Plot, was arrested while guarding explosives that the plotters had placed beneath the House of Lords.

In kind of the same fashion as America's Halloween and the ritual of the Trick or Treaters, the popular custom was to create a Guy Fawkes guy, complete with a body of newspapers wearing old jeans and a hat, similar to a scarecrow, put him in a wheel barrow and wheel him door to door, saying, "A penny for the Guy!" (Pennies were actually old English pennies, worth more, like a dollar each in those days.) Naturally, there was a lot of enjoyment for the kids to collect their "pennies"!

Well, it was fun for David and his buds to carry out this romping, but not quite fun enough for David's total pleasure! There came along one night when David decided to "be" the actual Guy! He dressed himself up in the Guy costume of jeans, a shirt, a hat and newspapers hanging in and out…put himself in the wheel barrow which his mates drove up to the first home on track. When the homeowner opened the front door, he looked precariously at David, the guy in disguise lying in the barrow. Even before the boys had a chance to say "A penny for the guy!", the man pulled out a knife, wielding it and proclaiming, "Well, what is this? Let's just see if this is the "Guy" or a real guy???!!!" In less than a second, David pounced out of the wheel barrow, leaping in full flight out of the yard and down the street with his "associates" fleeing right behind him!!!!! Needless to say, this was one scheme that never got repeated!!!

Another notable phenomenon, back to the nature of David and his buddies playing out their military shenanigans, occurred when the "troups" were pretending to demonstrate an ambush. In this particular episode, David's brother, James became involved. So, the combative four fearlessly engaged themselves at night in the thrill of being on the roof top of the local lingerie shop. This was big time craziness, and they were totally into it… not realizing how much more crazy it would become! All of a sudden, while prancing around on the roof, James fell through and landed on top of the lingerie display below! Oh my, this was a definite "get out of here right now!!!!!!!"…which they all did!!!

As Elaine relays each of these lively stories from her past as David, there is a "bouncy" look of exploding, hilarious surprise that sweeps across her face along with a bursting glint in her eyes that speaks for itself, "How did I ever do that???" And, every endeavor was unique within itself, with each new happening completely different from the last. Some were carefully planned out and others were totally spontaneous! Whether the plots got traced out or not, the driving incentive never waned.

Another great one, even though it ended in realization, became a huge "high", as the ultimate discovery came way long, in perspective, after the ongoing scheme unfolded! David and Wayne were the "perpetrators" on this one. The two set their sight on the local shoe store. The idea was to try to see how many shoes they could "confiscate" before they got caught!...absolutely no desire to steal…just to achieve the highest goal they could in removing shoes, one by one, by literally putting them on and wearing them out of the store!

The challenge lay ahead and for some time in good stead! Each boy put on each pair of shoes and proceeded to walk cautiously outside the store, wearing the new, "unbought" shoes. They then proceeded across the road to a grassy place next to a church and continued to load up a pile of their confiscations, one after the other.

At a consequential point, the shoe store "security personnel" discovered the game in progress, came over and gave them the "ultimatum"! At that stage, it didn't really matter, as David's goal had been to see how many shoes they could sequester and assemble! Well, there were over forty pairs of shoes!

Probably the most memorable devise was the go cart drive! David and his brother, James took four of the old big tires from the tractor trailer, hitched them onto a plank of wood and created the go cart of their dreams! David sat up front, steering, with James behind him. With no way to self power the cart, they knew to rely on the good ole hilly roads! And, they knew the best one was on Braintree Road. It had an up and down hill that led up to a really steep one, the biggest hill to be found! Off they went, anticipating the plunge downward! The plunge turned into a 60 mph plummet with a police car chasing them! As the police car caught up, driving along side of them, they gave them the riot act in warning of impending dangers! The looming danger became real when the go cart crashed into the fence of a nearby farm field and turned upside down. The officers made them walk all the way back home to the wrath of Dennis, who by that time had already been informed. Results? No more go carting!

Simple Joys

All naughtiness and nuttiness aside, there was something much more salient and satisfying for David, and that was the pure refreshment and mirth of the little enjoyments of life! It could be any ole thing, but whatever it was, David embraced it with utter happiness!

These simple joys were all around:

David was allowed to take up karate school along with his friends.

David enjoyed ring a ring o' roses, skipping, hop scotch, ball in the park, the swings, rounder's, cricket, tennis, racquetball, bowling, ping pong, pool, snooker, hide and seek, "You're it", and swimming at the local swimming pool in Braintree. (His friends taught him how to swim.)

Real winners were going to the movies, the circus, the fair grounds, and riding the dodgems.

David loved to go to the park in Coggeshall! There he adored performing on the swings, the monkey bars and the roundabout! He especially found fulfillment in talking to the occasional tramps and bringing them food and/or goodies.

He enjoyed riding push bikes all over the place! Since David and his pals were too young to own motorcycles, they used to "create" their own by inserting playing cards into the wheel spokes attached by wooden clothesline pegs to the bike wheel frame. This produced a "motorcycle" sound as the bike was being ridden, and David used to ride, either alone or with friends, and they got a charge out of racing down hills. One time David got a little too enthusiastic, and he decided to try to attach the lawnmower engine to his bike. It was okay…and worked for the first few seconds until the engine flew off the bicycle and wrapped around, cutting his leg…not something he wanted to try again!

It was super fun to swim in the river on the outskirts of Coggeshall. He also found comforting delight in catching fish in the river.

What a joy it was to capture apples and pears! This provided fun time for David and his pals, in scrumping for these fruits all around town, shaking their trees, collecting them and taking them away!

Catching lady bugs was continually a favorite, as was gathering the white fuzzy post dandelions! ("She loves me, She loves me not")

There were all sorts of creative outlets to be found in the fields on the farm:

After the corn was cut, it became a pastime with friends to pull up the stalks with mud root ends and throw them at each other! Ouch!

Then there was the diversion of taking the hay bales and building dens. The den became an imaginary house, complete all around from the rooftop to the front door. Lots of play went on here!

It was soothing sometimes to go into the hay sheds and just sit and hang out, singing songs!

Making English catapults and slinging them freely and safely out in the field or trying to hit cans and bottles was good sport!

Playing conkers was a real gaiety! David and his buddies would pick the conkers off the tree, split the outer shell to release the conker inside and then attach it to a string. The game engaged the challenge of swinging your conker against your playmate's conker, hitting as many times as it took until one broke! The Conker Champion was adulated, as it took a lot of ongoing might to break a conker...Conkers had a very hard consistency... tough stuff!

A wild and zippy experience was driving the motor bike, full speed all over the field! David and his group pitched in together and purchased a used Black Triumph 250 motor bike! It did not have a carburetor which allows for controlling how fast or slow you go, and no brakes to stop. But they didn't care, as they were taking it for a free ride instant at full speed in the open field! So, the petrol was poured in to the head of the engine, and off they went...one at a time, on a barbarous high speed ride through the field, up and down and all around, in highest acceleration until the fuel eventually ran out. A thrill beyond belief!

A huge delight for David was trekking to the local sweet shop to wallow in all the sweetness and to pick out his beloved treats to purchase! Having saved up his old English pennies from toil here and there, now was the time to savor!!! So many goodies to choose from!...

But David knew his most desired little "pets"!!! Bon Bons, either toffee, chocolate, strawberry or vanilla were high on the list! Right next to them came the lemon drops, black jacks, flying saucers with sherbert, licorice sticks, gob stoppers, chewing gum, bubble gum and fruit salad sweets! Last but not least, the chocolate round bites, milk chocolate or white chocolate, with what seemed like "thousands" of tasty colored sprinkles on top!

Every so often, David could not afford to buy his savored candied treasures. No problem! He would just go to the pet store and buy the dog "chocks" and eat 'em up!!! Not a bad price and not a bad taste!!! Elaine swears to this day that this experience is why she has such soft and shiny skin!)

It was also fun as an early child to hang out at home with Dora and James, whether it was watching movies, TV programs, playing cards, Monopoly, Checkers, telling jokes or heading down to the off license in the local pub to buy sweets, crisps and soft drinks. Walking back home along Tey Road could be pitch black and quite scary, and it was always a welcome relief to get back to the house! Dora used to often bring boxes of chocolates home, and the three kids would relish eating them up! On some nights, they would partake in fish 'n chips, pasties and pies. These were the simple days when everything was normal.

Elaine has very fond memories of many times going to visit a school friend whose family lived in Kelvedon, three and a half miles away. David always felt a welcome calm being there, and he was treated as a family member. Elaine remembers the refreshment of eating wonderful homemade meals and watching exciting movies on the television. It was usually an overnight stay, which was ceaselessly enjoyable!

A special gladness was "playing groupie" at another school mate's house in Coggeshall on certain weekends. The band of the day would play in their barn, and David got a bang out of helping them set up and participating in the fun!

David always found contentedness in relationships! It started as a young dapper kid and would continue throughout his life. At age seven, feeling more like a girl than a boy, he/she had a boyfriend named Anthony. Their romance entailed kissing in the cornfields! In his early teens, he became enraptured with Peggy! They would go on long walks, holding hands and hang out just about everywhere in Coggeshall. At age thirteen, David met Susan in Braintree, and in keeping with these simple romantic joys, the two of them found lightheartedness in sitting on the park bench, talking and kissing.

A real favorite pastime was hanging out with the local tramp, who lived by the tree in the park. David and the boys would bring him food, and the tramp relished in telling the kids his real life stories from his days of being a soldier and becoming shell shocked! The guys also found pleasure in keeping company with the hippies who took up shelter in the abandoned homes in the village. They enjoyed the thrill of being around the friendly dissenters who captivated them with their guitar playing and musical spouts, ranting against war and for peace!!!

David had a steadfast infatuation for music! Ever since he was a wee child, he undyingly adored to listen to songs and sing them! Elaine affectionately remembers when, as David, his mum bought him his first 45 record, "Old McDonald Had a Farm" and then later his second treasure, "Living Doll". Since sister, Dora was the one who had a record player in her bedroom, he memorably would pounce into her room when she was out and immerse himself in the repetitive sounds that never failed to captivate him! He indulged in playing Dora's records too, as well as a few of his mum's! He loved to sing along with every note and never wanted it to end! A special gratification was to switch a 45 to a 78 higher speed and sing it up, rockin' with the sound on a faster track!

One time, David was so proud and filled up with his expressive and creative sounds that he bounced downstairs in musical delight and put on his own little show, singing and dancing for Mildred and Dennis! He reenacted a slow song to a faster rock n' roll pace, but before he got a chance for his splash of an ending, Dennis cut him off, saying, "Stop it, you're not original!...Elvis Presley sings and dances like that! You and Elvis can't sing, and neither of you will last very long!"

David hadn't given much attention to Elvis at all aside from hearing his name spoken. But later on, when he caught a glimpse of Elvis doing his act on television, David inquired to his mom, "Hey, Mum, how come someone can do the same thing as me? How will I ever be original?" David danced like Elvis and had a natural vibrato in his voice delivery that sounded just like Elvis. David's mum just smiled.

Shortly after, Elaine has a poignant memory of David being confused and frustrated, feeling that his voice was somehow wrong, and therein going out and walking down the street, trying to sing out in another way that was different. But every time he tried, the altered voice was definitely not his and certainly did not feel right! It was forced and not intrinsic! As a stricken result, Dennis refused to let David have music lessons, which he so badly wanted to have! David used to watch through the little window of the door at school as his classmates learned music, played piano and guitar. This made David feel extremely sad and left out.

Out And Beyond

In living under the problematic circumstances of his mum's demise and the ongoing fighting between Dennis and Mildred, in the summer of David's thirteenth year, he broke out and ran away to Great Yarmouth on the sea. This was a popular seaside town. David had spent some weekends there before with his buddies, and so he knew it well and was very familiar with the surroundings. It was known for its alluring amusement park, and that is where David gained work! He sold tickets to the rides and also was in charge of starting up and stopping the various rides. He basically roughed it by hanging out on the streets and by finding a sleeping spot on the beach or at a hotel.

David got a lot of pleasure in entering a singing competition at a local hotel. He sang his original children's song, "I Love You" and won second place! Moving along, David got a kick out of entertaining and singing rock n' roll songs while shaking his hips for tourists at hotels.

All in all, David found a satisfying niche in being a "Teddy Boy"!

This was definitely "the thing"!!! It was an animate part of an evolution, raised out of the depression and the invention of Rock N' Roll in the 50's and 60's.

Being a Teddy Boy was one of five essential components of this phenomenon:

Rockers: These were hard core Rock N' Roll bikers! They wore leather jackets and blue jeans. Some had tattoos.

Teddy Boys: They were Rock N' Rollers, wore blue suede shoes, had fashioned hair and clothes of the Fifties. Some had tattoos.

Mods: These guys were funky Scooters, looking modern in their suits, etc. They wore long parker coats, nice shoes, and they had professional haircuts.

Punk Rocker: Lovers of hard punk rock music, these dudes had safety pins in their nose, mouth and ears and definitely tattoos! They had multi colored hair that sticks up and they flaunted colorful clothing.

Skin Heads: With shaved heads, these dudes wore blue jeans, many times turned up at the bottom, and black steel toe boots. They carried flick knives, hard and tough, and they were known as Head Bangers.

David discovered that he perfectly fitted the image of the "Teddy Boy"!

Whether he was on the street, roaming around, hanging out on the beach, playing the penny arcade, or going to the rock n' roll dance clubs, David had a natural, suave way of engaging with folks of all kinds! In teddy boy antics, he would smoothly pull out his comb from his back pocket, giving a straight boy look, curling his lip, and sleekly combing his hair!!!

At the end of that summer, David returned to his home in Coggeshall and his school life at Honeywood. On the weekends, and some weeknights, he reluctantly became a part of the Army Cadets in the town of Braintree, west of Coggeshall, about eight miles away. Whether it was for four hours in the late afternoon and evening, or for a whole day, it was a disciplinary routine on which Dennis insisted…real hard physical training and constant body testing. David would either take the bus or ride the bike back and forth. This became an ongoing strain for him along with the other elements of his environmental issues. Nevertheless, David prevailed.

Unbeknownst to David and James at the time, Dennis had been living out an affair with Minnie, the wife of Dennis' helper that he had hired to do the extra logging on the weekends. The boys eventually found out that this secret relationship had been going for quite some time. Dora had already moved out of the house. She had been working as a hairdresser in town when she met Jake. They got married. Jake was in the army based at the Barracks in Colchester. He and she moved on to Germany, where Jake was to serve his four-year required stint. Dora followed in Dennis and Mildred's footsteps and lived in the barracks with Jake in Germany.

Meanwhile, Mildred's condition was sadly only continuing to go downhill. Dennis never offered to provide her help. For some time and progressively, Mildred had been dipping into the grocery money to pay for her beer. This made Dennis more and more angry, and he would yell at her! When he became too fed up with the situation, he would take his army backpack and bicycle to the bus stop, then taking a bus into Colchester to buy a week's load of food. (There were many times that David felt sorry for Dennis, and this was one of them…seeing him carry a full backpack after a hard day at work. It was soul destroying! And then, to see the decline of food that Mildred used to cook was sending out more signs of her downward spiral.)

David really never knew Dennis as a father or a person because he spent most of his life being afraid of him. And, Dennis was always hostile towards David. David had lots of ideas and lots of dreams, and not once did he ever try to support him. He just aggressively was negative and non supportive of anything that David tried to do. David never, ever had a conversation with this "father". What made it even more confusing was…Was there another Dennis that David did not know?…As, for example, after David's surgery, on the doctor's recommendation, he bought David a dog, a black collie that David named Blackie. He was his best friend, and they spent years of good times together, with David even sleeping at times with Blackie in his kennel.

There were other times that David saw glimpses of Dennis' human side. One of them was in regards to the fact that Dennis used to collect exotic birds, and he had an aviary in the back yard where he used to tend to the birds. One time, David caught seeing him praying and crying in the aviary. So, who was this man? David did not know, and he would never know.

Dennis, Mildred and David used to usually sit at the kitchen table together around 5 PM. It was confusing for David, as here they were trying to live a family life, but Dennis was always so irate at not only Mildred but at David! And David could not figure out why! Naturally, David was constantly terrified when sitting at the dinner table, in not knowing what to expect.

At one point, Mildred and Dennis had another more dramatic fight, and Dennis ruthlessly threw her out on the street! He gave her $50.00 cash, and that was it! Soon after, he moved Minnie, his mistress into the house.

Mildred, emotionally, mentally and physically destroyed after so many years, used the money to catch a train to Taunton in Somerset where she found refuge with her mother.

David was ravaged by the whole ordeal, in not only listening to the loud and bitter argument, but in watching his mom being thrown out of the front door. He stood at the open door, yelling out at her, "Mum, I love you! I'll come and see you!!!"

Beyond question, the absence of David's mum in the home was crucially hard and trying on him. It became increasingly difficult to be in the house with Dennis without his mother. There was a very bad vibe permeating the surroundings! Clearly, Dennis did not want him there, and at the same time, David felt trapped!

Looking back, David was always made to feel that there was something wrong with him and that everything was all of his fault. David constantly battled trying to understand this father figure. He never allowed David be close enough to get to know him. David felt that this life growing up was the way it was supposed to be, as he had nothing to compare it with. And, thus David thought that because he was treated as the "bad kid" and that nothing that he did was right and that he never fitted into the family, he assumed that something about himself was really wrong and that he didn't truly belong.

When David turned fourteen, his school decided that it would be beneficial for his best progress and more technical learning to send him to the Alec Hunter School in Braintree, eight miles from Coggeshall. He took the bus every day back and forth. That was a good part school year for David. He got a lot out of his tenure there and really got into his courses.

That summer, David ran away to South End On Sea, about 35 miles south by the ocean. David worked jobs there at the big amusement park, just as he had done in Great Yarmouth years earlier.

When David came back home after about a month, Dennis said, "What did you come back for?" Dennis in fury and impediment consequently set up a meeting in the local court to persuade the judge to legally have David sent away. In remembrance of that awful day, Elaine relives David's emotions of shock, dejection and devastation…not to mention the horror of deceit by Dennis: He told the judge that David had become too much of a burden, stemming back to when he implied that his son had stolen items from the farm owners. (which was an outright lie...Dennis had done that himself!)

As it turned out, there was no question that the judge had sympathy for David. He could tell that David was not a thief or criminal of any sorts. But he had to make the best decision for David's future, and he knew that Dennis had no desire to keep him. Under the circumstances, the judge had no choice but to make arrangements for David to be moved to Boyle's Court, a children's convalescence home and school, located in the town of Brentwood, Essex. (An important fact to mention here is that Dennis gave both Dora and James the inheritance of a trust insurance policy benefit, along with full family, love, care and support. Yet David received none.)

After this horrible proclamation, Dennis and David walked to a room next to the courtroom where David blared out to his uncaring dad, "Why are you doing this to me???" Dennis said, "I love you, but I cannot look after you anymore. This is for your own good, and I want you to know that you can never come back." (This harsh and cold response set up with the false feeling of love was obviously meant to settle David's wrath and resentment, so that the process could move forward without any complications.) David quickly reacted, "No, you don't love me!...You set me up!!!"

An important point to realize here is that in regard to this impactful situation, there were two sides to this coin on behalf of David's feelings towards Dennis. He was torn between conflicting sentiments! He naturally disliked and abhorred the way Dennis maltreated him, but on the other hand, he felt a certain sort of allegiance to him as his "dad", as he was the only dad he had ever known, and, as noted before, in his mind, this was supposed to be "normal. He grew to understand that this is the way it was supposed to be, and he wanted to believe, as his son, that Dennis cared for him.

Following this distressful confrontation, David was escorted to a van outside where the driver met him. The destination was Boyles Court. During the unsettling drive ahead, David's heavy thoughts ran wild... "Dennis had thrown Mildred out. Now he is throwing me out. Who is this man? He is supposed to be my father, yet I realize more than ever that I never ever knew him!"

A New Beginning

Upon arrival at Boyles Court, David was amazed over how very beautiful the grounds were. The long road, called Dark Lane was lined with massive trees that made a continuous arch over the lane. At the end of the lane, there was a white house where the manager lived. Going up a long windy driveway from there, the enormously spread out mansion in the distance ahead became closer and closer. It appeared to David to be a castle! After thanking the driver and saying "Goodbye!", David was taken to the front reception office. He was immediately impressed with the warm welcome! He was given clothes: blue jeans, shirts and a preferential red, blue and white checkered flannel jacket. Then he sat down to listen to the strong but essential words from the Director:

"What I'm going to tell you will be hard, but you are here to stay. It would be unhealthy for you to go back. Most kids who are with us come here to get reestablished so that they can eventually go back home. In your case, you are better off to stay here. If you should ever go back home, it would be too unstable for you. You are here so that we can help you, and we will help you in the best way that we can.

I also am here to inform you that your dad, Dennis Mower is not your real father. Under the circumstances, it is recommended that you not only do not return to him, but also not to your mother." (In David's mind, after that powerful statement regarding Dennis being his false dad, he deciphered that the reason for this news was to protect him after all that he had been through.)

David was soon taken to his living quarters, a shared large room with bunk beds. After unpacking his bag and getting a feel of his new environment, he was given a tour of the children's home before arriving at the dining room for dinner. During the tour, it was personally explained to David that this setting was not a prison or punishment place for him, but rather a home! The fact was made clear that there were two distinct groups of kids. The ones living downstairs, including David, were the "good guys". The ones living on the upper level were the "bad guys", the troubled boys who had histories of everything from

mental illness to criminal minds to potential endangerment to themselves and/or others.

In the first couple of days, David began to gradually process his feelings of the "homesick" jolt of the whole happening soon to be surpassed by the realization of relief and the new understanding of the meaning of what "normal" was all about!

In the following several weeks, he emerged into the significant comprehension that he no longer felt useless or worthless! He realized more and more that this was what feeling normal meant and that he never did have a normal life before! Now, he actually had worth and value! There was no more stress or fear, and he suddenly felt free!

(And the longer that David lived out his tenure at Boyles Court, the more he embraced the reality of his merit, caliber and goodness.)

Jumping right into the throes and realities of existing in this home for boys, David met another new kid named Kevin. Kevin looked up to David as he could tell that he was a good guy. But at the same time, he was jealous of David for being so handsome and "straight arrow". One day, Kevin decided to pick a fight with David. He wanted to put David to the test! He had been bullying him for a couple of days ahead of this skirmish. David easily won, in wrestling him to the ground. Kevin never picked a fight again with David. And in fact, the two ended up becoming best friends!

Two other guys befriended David along the way, and there was a strong sense of brotherhood between them. David had a certain defined aura about him with his "pretty" looks, natural shyness and "genuineness". David's "brothers" very well liked to look after him. They told David that he was like their little "dollie". They treated him with kindness and niceness. One of the boys used to enjoy styling David's hair.

All of the boys at Boyles Court spent time doing hard labor on the grounds, digging trenches in the ground, planting trees, etc. But David was lucky. He was never assigned to any sort of these duties. Yet, David was given the special responsibility of retrieving the kids who tried to run away and then talking with each one of them, in helping to make them feel better. David energetically took on this job with a natural fit and great satisfaction!

An unforgettable experience for David at Boyles Court was in the making. On this significant occasion, David was asked to come to the front office. He was told that, as a special child in a unique spot from the norm, they did not designate jobs for him, as the other boys who toiled in their regimen.

But now they presented David with a very important job and mission. Since he had a track record of successfully bringing back runaway kids and helping them, it was decided to elevate David to a calling on the upper level, the high security floor of the home, where boys were in conditions of mental disorders and major instabilities. As proven, David had a natural way with talking to kids, easing their tensions, settling them down and bringing them out! David was grateful for this well deserved "promotion", but he also knew that there carried with it a possible risk and danger factor.

Most of these boys were extremely unstable with intricate issues, and David took on this challenging mission with determination and dedication. One of the boys named Freddy was in a very fragile state and suicidal. David treated his visits with him very seriously and carefully. Fred was in a stupor much of the time. He would constantly stare at walls with no reaction or feeling. David wanted so badly to break through this dilemma and get through to him with constant reassurance and kind patience. But words did not seem to matter a whole lot. David engaged him with games, such as playing cards. Freddy could play, and often he could beat David, but it did not seem to go anywhere with any results. A couple of times, Freddy started to be violent by jumping out of his chair and lunging toward David, but in David's alertness and in thanks to help from staff, it was averted.

Certain boys, as well as David, on the main level received a weekly allowance, which they received on Fridays. Then when Saturdays came along, these were the fun days for these happy boys! Usually about twelve of them piled into the Boyles Court van early in the morning for their all day lively spree in the town of Brentwood, about two miles down the road. They called the driver "Cowboy", and they felt it was a real wild time!

After a week or so, David discerned that this weekly ride was way too boring for all of them, especially in earnest and restless anticipation of getting there! So, on one of the first journeys, David engaged in the spontaneous inventive thrill of dreaming up a sort of theme song for the boys to sing! The "Boyles Court Song". It was the perfect solution and ongoing musical chant that satisfied everyone! The boys loved it and learned it quickly! It became a joyous ritual for all of them to sing their theme song, and to sing it out loudly, on every trip to town and back!

And, here is David's song:

Boyles Court Song

Eggs and bacon we don't' see

We get sawdust in our tea

That's why we're slowly fading away!

At six o'clock in the morning

We hear the cowboy shout

"Get out of bed, get out of bed

Before you get a clout!

He wraps us in a blanket

He chucks us in the van

The van is very bumpy

We nearly tumble out!

And when we get to Boyles Court

We hear the children shout

"Mummy, Daddy, take me home

From this convalescent home…

I've been here a year or two

Now I want to be with you!

We hear the children shout

"Stay there, you bastards, stay there, you bastards

We don't want you no more!

Stay there, you bastards

We don't want you no more

Stay there, you bastards

We don't want you no more

Stay there, you bastards

We don't want you no more!"

When in town, there was much play perpetually awaiting! Everything from shopping for anything from 45 records to t shirts to having lunch to going to the movies! Fun all the way around!

And, then there was Linda. David met her in town on one of the early Saturday ventures. It was an automatic attraction. Linda worked in the local jewelry store. David used to go to the bus stop and walk her to work. During her lunch break, David was always there to be there with her, and they loved every minute of it! After her work day and David's day in town, David would typically walk her back to the bus stop.

Sometimes, about twice a month, David was given the privilege of coming back home with Linda to spend the night. He regularly savored his stays there, and Linda's parents were very good to him, treating him wonderfully, as a future son-in-law! They would always make scrumptious homemade meals, allowing David to help out in the preparation and cooking process. Linda's dad made homemade beer, and he engaged David in showing him his method and giving him taste tests. David delighted in that!

In the following mornings after a family breakfast, Linda used to typically walk David to the bus stop where he would go back to Brentwood and then walk back to Boyles. It was always a brisk and very happy walk, as David was re-living his memorable visit and feeling very much in love!

On one of those valued day and night visitations, David proposed marriage to Linda sitting on a bench in town. He was feeling dapper wearing a smart black jacket, and she was lovely in her pretty dress. The two were mesmerized in happiness, especially when Linda said, "Yes!" When they arrived at her folk's home, the news broke into joyous celebration! Linda's parents told them later that because they were engaged, it was alright for them to sleep in the same bedroom together. Oh, Boy!!!

A Turn Around and a Hard Turn

Approximately a year and a half to two years after David first entered Boyles Court, the time period came when several boy residents qualified for going back home to their families. At this point in time, David had a natural curiosity as to what was going on at his old place and how it might turn out if he went back there. He was taken to the main office to discuss this proposition. David was told that it was not a good decision and that they were very concerned about his well being. But if he still wanted to go, they would allow him to do it. Yet, it was made clear that if things did not turn out, he would always be made welcome to come back to Boyles Court!

The return to the old home was definitely not a good thing! What an eye opening event! Before two days were up, David was on his way back to Boyles Court!

During his quick and uncomfortable stay, David was handled with no "handlement" at all! False father, Dennis and presumably brother, James were very cold, almost acting as if David was not even there!

While there, David smoked one of Dennis's cigars. James told Dennis about this "heinous" event, and that was the kicker for Dennis throwing David out of the house!

In defying revenge, David took off and drove the mini cooper (that he had bought for 50 dollars) all over the corn field near the property, crying out in wild retaliation and enjoying every time the corn hit the windshield! After his revengeful glee, he was "off and running" for the eight and a half mile walk to the train station to take the train back to Brentwood and then the two mile walk back to Boyles Court.

In arriving back at Boyles Court, as he walked down the long driveway, he was spotted by a bunch of "Boyles Courters" with enthusiasm! "Hey, you're back! Welcome back!!!" In entering the main office, he was submerged in tears. The manager/counselor said, "Don't feel bad, just don't ever do it again!"

David was more than relieved to be back! He now truly understood why he had always felt so happy in living at Boyles Court. It was a comfort and revitalization to be back in the old familiar routine!...until...

About three months down the road, a new kid made his ominous entrance into the home. David B. Another David, but not quite the same as David Mower!!! Not one single bit! He proved in a short time that he was not only not anywhere near an ordinary boy, but the hardest, toughest, meanest kid ever to come to Boyles Court!

When the new David met the former David, it was a wild confrontation about to happen! David B. became aware right away of Mower's attributes in good looks and engaging personality. It became evident that he wanted to be the other David, as he would invariably ask the other boys if he looked like him. Or, he would ask if the two looked like brothers. The response he usually got was "Oh, yeah, yeah, ya do!", as they were afraid of him!

In several instances to come, the "Bad David" beat up the "Good David", and in each situation, it was a threatening aftermath with David B. saying, "If you tell on me, I will beat you up again!"

David's time living at Boyles Court was about to come to an end in January, not long after his 16th birthday in December. There became an availability for two boys to be in foster care at a private home in South End On Sea. The home owners were government social workers who provided "half way house" opportunities for those in need. They already had two boys in residence, and now there would be two more!

Unbelievably, the other boy besides David that was sent to this new abode was the other David! Needless to say, David Mower was petrified in the knowledge and experience of this, knowing how menacing David could be!

David found a job right away working full time at a car factory in South End On Sea making the black visors that were part of the rear windows of Ford Capris. On Saturdays, the four boys would usually take the train to town to goof around. On one of the train treks, mean David engrossed in a despicable act on David. He tortuously yanked David to the outside train door where he forcibly and wrenchingly hung David halfway out the open door, twice yanking him quickly back in, and then out again, as David's head and body barely missed, within seconds, the oncoming steel posts. David was unspeakably ravaged by this horrendous and desecrating perversion! The "Executioner David" was even shaken by it all. The "Victim David" came so very close to death. This wretched act never happened again.

Held in Hell

David longingly ached for the weekend to come around, usually twice a month, when he could take the train in South End On Sea to Brentwood, walk to the bus stop and take the bus to see Linda.

On one of these Saturdays, David was happily into his walk, eagerly anticipating the joy of being with his girl, when a police car pulled up next to him in Brentwood on High Street. The officer said, "Hi, how are ya doing?" David said that he was fine, just going to his girlfriend's place. The officer replied, "Would you mind going to the station with me? Just want to ask you a few questions." David asked, "Why?" The officer said that it wasn't much…just a few questions and then they'd let him go…

Once at the station, they took David's fingerprints without saying a word. Then David was given jail clothes and put in a cell. Startlingly, David pleaded, "What the hell is going on???" He was told that he was going back to South End On Sea. He was under arrest.

After spending a horrible night in the jail cell, two detectives came in the next day to take David back to South End On Sea and place him in the police station there. On the way in the police vehicle, David kept saying again, "What the heck is going on here?" He was given no answers, and it seemed obvious that the detectives were being as "nice" as they could be in order to prep David for what was to come.

Upon arriving at the station there, David was given different jail clothes and then was put in his "newest" jail cell. He was to spend two days at this next calamitous venue. Two or three times a day, he was taken upstairs to a room where he was vigorously interrogated by two detectives as to what had happened. There was the "good guy", the nice detective and the "bad guy", the mean detective. Becoming more and more scared and confused, David repeatedly cried out, "Tell me what this is all about! I have no idea what is going on!"

A form was placed on the table in front of him, and David was asked to sign it. David refused. In ongoing intimidating attempts to try to make David sign the form, he never let up in refusing and never let up in pleading to have an answer about what was the nature of all this harrassment ! This only brought on the provocation for the "bad guy" detective to hassle him even more! "Admit it! You know you did it!", he shouted! David's rejection held on. The verbal reaction that resulted was a nonstop, battering that relentlessly never seemed to end. "If you sign it now, you can go home!" No matter how drained and ravaged he was, David knew better… "No!"

On the second day of this hellish experience, a doctor was brought in to take DNA scrapings on David's body. He was told that they would have all the evidence from the doc and that when it came back "positive", he would have a lot longer sentence than if he'd just sign the document right away, allowing him a lot less sentence! David didn't buy it! No way!

Thus, the form was shoved in front of him again and again with more and more demands to sign it! Completely exhausted and overwhelmed, David begged for the "millionish" time again, "What the heck is all this about???" He finally got a response: "You murdered her. Sign it!"

Angry beyond belief and totally worn down, David looked up at the officers and announced, "What the fuck!" He was consequently thrust back into his cell, and David became even more terrified!

About two hours later, an officer came to David's cell and opened the door. He said, "Get dressed!" With that, he left the cell door open. Hours later, while David was still sitting in his cell wearing his regular clothes and waiting with the door still wide open, the two detectives came and stated, "Follow us." After escorting him outside, David was told, "You are free to go. But if you ever say anything about what happened here, then we will never leave you alone!"

In Elaine's re-living of this three-day traumatic experience from hell for David, it is very, very painful and extremely discomforting, not only in the awful memory of dealing with it, but in the anguish of realizing again how wrongfully and dishonestly the whole thing was handled! In essence, David was kidnapped, lied to and tortured by the police!

When David was released, he was in such tormented shape, emotionally, mentally and physically that he really should have been hospitalized. He wandered around in residual shock and complete depletion before he finally took the long walking trek back to his adoptive home in the suburbs of South End On Sea. In recollection, it had to have been a sheer survival mechanism that kicked into gear!

David soon discovered the reality surrounding the course of these unusual events. It was a big story all over the news. A woman had been murdered in her South End On Sea home. David was just one of many possible suspects that had been confiscated in regard to this tragedy. All three of David's roommates were victims of this calamity as well.

The upcoming Saturday, David was more than exuberant to go back to visit Linda at her family's place. They were, at the least, ecstatic to see him! It was wonderful to receive their consolation and understanding concerning what David had been through. It felt good for a bit with Linda, but then a certain sense of "something different" set in.

On that following Sunday when David would normally return home after a Saturday night stay with Linda, he was afraid to go back, in paranoia that the police in South End On Sea would come and get him for something else! David asked Linda's parents if he could stay over for another night or two. They told him that it was important that he get back to his "kid in care" residence. Otherwise, it could mean legal trouble for both parties, Linda's parents and David's adoptive parents.

Nonetheless, David was allowed to spend the next two nights there, but it was arranged for him to stay in their shed. Linda's family was very much aware of the fragility of David's condition, and they wanted to help him as much as they could without jeopardizing all involved.

But, they made David aware that he must not stay there any longer after that due to the fact that they could possibly be arrested for kidnapping!

Despite this awkward situation, Linda's folks had an unbroken affection for David. They wanted very much for him to stay with their daughter. But apparently Linda had other thoughts and was moving in another direction. She felt that David's circumstances were too unstable. Her parents vehemently said, "No! None of any of this was David's fault!" Meanwhile, she had started dating Max, the manager of the jewelry store where she worked. Seemingly, Linda felt there would be more security with him.

David and Linda walked to the bus stop for their final goodbye. It was snowing, and the snowflakes seemed to carry a stinging pelting rather than an aura of romance. Even though they still held hands and kissed and said to each other, "Love you!", there was to be a new walk on a new path ahead for both of them.

Linda tenderly yet decisively expressed to David that she had chosen to leave the relationship. "After all that you have been through, it's just too much for me to handle." She told him that she was seeing Max and that she felt he could take better care of her. One last hug and kiss…They never saw each other again…

Nowhere Lies Ahead

When David came back to his adoptive home in South End On Sea, the parents and the boys were very, very happy to see him, but there were restrictions that followed. Because David had spent time over his allowed time away, he was given a firm curfew, in that for the next two weeks, he could not go anywhere in that duration, except for to his job.

But soon after that time period, David dreaded coming back home from work on the workday evenings, as the "Bad David" was always trying to coax him into going along with the other boys to town at night to rob the local candy factory. (They successfully did this many times, bringing home their huge load of treasured snow balls!...a spongy kind of cake with chocolate and coconut on the outside.) David always resisted having any part of it except for one time when he felt uneasy about being threatened, and in that episode, David went along but only stayed in the background watching it all unfold.

Due to David's resistance to this criminal caper, the "Bad David" felt compelled to take it out on him. One night at the house, he snuck in to David's room and forcefully placed the pillow on his head, trying to suffocate him. Thankfully, one of the other "good guys" saw this happening and saved him!

David went into deep shock. By the time he recovered in four days, thankfully and amazingly, David's foster parents had secured another home for him. This was an emergency adoption and became the fastest adoption in UK history!

The new adoptive parents were a married couple, Sandy and Jeff. Sandy was more than happy to take David in, as she knew him from the workplace. Sandy was the accountant at the car factory where David worked. She had a liking for David since he first came to the job.

Sandy and Jeff had a small house on the outskirts of South End On Sea, not far from the car factory. They were both very nice and friendly with David. Jeff was a long-distance truck driver, and he would ordinarily be gone on a stretch for several days. From the beginning, Sandy was acting with flirtation toward David, and without David saying anything, it became apparent that he had no interest in her at all. David was already involved with Jeannette, the secretary at the car place. Sandy ultimately figured it all out and started treating David with a cold distance.

One day, while on his way walking back home from work, a policeman in plain clothes approached David. He asked some basic questions about David's situation living with the couple. Then he told David to be aware, as he said. "These people you are living with are not who they seem to be! Be CAREFUL!"

About three weeks later, when the folks were gone, David was fixing dinner in the kitchen and was looking in the drawers to find a utensil. In one of the drawers, he was stunned to find a gun! It was a handgun.

In curiosity, he very carefully picked up the gun and took it with him to the woods for about ten minutes to test it out and see how it worked! David shot it out twice high over a tree! It scared him a lot, not only due to the loudness and impact, but to the fear of potential endangerment! He quickly came back home and placed the gun in its original place!

(In England at that time, it was illegal for anyone to have guns.)

Close to a week after this frightful incident, David discovered Sandy crying profusely one night! She was distraught over the fact that Jeff had been arrested for not only drug dealing but for drug trafficking! This was a much more serious crime. Jeff was in jail.

Amazingly, after two weeks, he got out of his confines and came back home. Almost immediately, Jeff came to David and emphatically told him. "If anybody asks you any questions about this, don't say anything!" Terrified, David went to his room, sat on the bed and indulged in deep logical thought amidst his frightened brain. He knew that being a regular drug dealer was one thing, but being heavily involved in the transport of big chunks of drugs from one location to another was a huge other dangerous deal.

David realized that suddenly now he was in an extremely hazardous situation. Due to the unstable volatility of these circumstances, he could easily be killed by Jeff or any of the persons with whom he was dealing!

David had no choice but to get out as soon as he could! After quitting his job with his bag already packed, David took to the streets…

It was winter, and that season in England can be miserably cold and brutal. Not a good time to be without a place to stay! In his bare minimum of clothing and only one coat, David found himself being homeless. In anxious need for survival, he resorted to finding refuge by sneaking inside people's unlocked cars in their driveways and huddling in the back seat, trying to sleep. He soon succumbed to miserable frost bite and big warts on his legs.

When daylight came, even on a sunny day, he still felt so very freezing and was constantly shaking! He pushed himself as much as he could to do walking, walking, and more walking and trying to run in order to get his circulation going and to feel at least a little rebirth of warming.

This horrid ordeal lasted for about a week, and fortunately David was able to get enough cash out of his last paycheck to make it nutritionally.

With every bit of fortitude that he could muster, David embarked on the train to Bristol. He went to the government office there and requested assistance. Thankfully, they gave him money, food and accommodation at a room to rent for about ten days while he looked for employment. Unfortunately, as hard as he tried, David could not find a job.

Mum's The Way

Despite these setbacks, David set his mind on moving forward with a yearning and a plan. He decided at this crossing that it was the ideal and much needed timing for him to go visit his precious mother, Mildred. He had longed to do this for the longest time since Dennis had sent her away from the house in Coggeshall. But he was restricted for a lengthy period, from being in custody of Dennis, to Dennis throwing him into the children's home at age 14, to being sent to foster homes at 16 to running away and becoming homeless and "in the wild".

At this volatile point, after getting off the streets, David was finally free! He jumped on the springboard to take the train to Somerset where his mum lived in a one bedroom flat on the top floor at 84 Creech Barrow Road, in Taunton. He stayed with her there for two months, while working two jobs, cooking chicken at a restaurant on Taunton High Street for the first month and then clearing and cleaning tables at a motorway restaurant, about a mile down the road.

On his days off, David particularly relished his private times, venturing across the street to the field with his black guitar where he would dream up his own songs and play them, singing to the universe!

Mildred's mother, known as Nan to David, lived about a thousand feet down the street from his mom's place. He especially loved walking with his mum down to visit her, which they did quite often! David very much fancied being at his grandmother's house, chatting with her and enjoying a cup of tea.

Elaine affectionately calls to mind, as David, when Nan told him passionately again what she had expressed to him as a child…that he was very, very special, and that he did not belong to Dennis! Nan never wanted Mildred to be with Dennis. She wished her daughter had stayed away from Dennis, as he was not a good man.

David knew all too well that his mum was a major alcoholic. It was evident that she drank everyday. She had the habit of going to see Nan,

going shopping and going drinking. Regardless of what anyone said, Mildred was stubborn and did what she wanted, not considering the consequences. Occasionally, David and his mom would venture to the nearby pub for relaxation. David was well aware, in his own knowledge and from hearing from everyone around, that he should not buy her more than one drink and/or not to give her any money for alcohol. (Mildred liked drinking half pints of Guinness.)

It became more and more clear that David's mum had deep mental problems and disturbingly continued to not go for help. Instead, she drank to relieve her mental stress. Elaine, as David, brings back vivid contrasting memories of his mom being a striking, young woman with brunette hair, caringly preparing food in the kitchen… to becoming an unstable lady with grey and white hair, sitting at the kitchen table with food on herself, rocking back and forth.

Yet, after all of this transformation and despite Mildred being in deep pain, David was astounded over how much of an angelic look she retained, even without bathing and having no makeup.

In a very sad and shaking recall, David tried desperately to encourage his mum to bathe and to get her into the bathtub. This became a huge effort, and things seemed to be progressing. But before even getting one of her feet into the bath, Mildred started screaming and shouting and pushing David away! Being that she was so used to originally being so sophisticated and dignified, the sheer thought of someone trying to help her in this state, combined with her obvious mental and drinking problems, was just too much for her to deal with! David was distraught and destroyed over not being able to help his mom, even taking into consideration that his Nan had said over and over that her daughter would simply not get help of any kind.

That same evening, David's mum suggested that he get his own place to live. Apparently, she sensed that he was trying to put her in the hospital. Despairingly, he agreed. As David walked to the door to say "Goodbye", they were both deeply crying. Elaine intensely remembers, as David, hugging his mum at least ten times before he walked down the front steps. As he descended, he looked back, and their eyes stayed locked. As he slowly went out of sight, he shouted "I love you, Mum!!!"

This was the climactic point in David's life when he thought his mother had abandoned him, even though he knew that she was very ill. This whole sorrowful experience brought David's memory back to when the manager at the children's home, Boyle's Court strongly advised him to never go back and visit either one of his parents again. In light of this misfortune with Mildred combined with the earlier shocking impression with Dennis, for many years David could not shake the pressing feeling of being abandoned by both parents.

As David was walking down the road, he didn't really comprehend the dangers of his situations. Here he was, barely an adult with only fifty pounds in his pocket, hitching a lift to London. Elaine now swears to God that angels must have been looking after him, as David, as the whole situation at that time was extremely dangerous. She remembers thinking that his mother was allowing him to do this. But he also was aware that she did not understand about the possible consequences in which she had placed him. He profoundly was bringing back to mind that during this last visit with his mum, she had mentioned to him that there was something important that she wanted to tell him some day and that she would tell him later on when he was older. (This affirmation, coupled with the intensity of the comments that his grandmother had already made in regards to David being special, really stirred David's curiosity of this mystery.)

The Road Opens

Determined, David hitched a ride to London where for a long and homeless week, he sought work. Along the way, he was invariably being pursued by street drug dealers to buy their heroine, but David never succumbed as he was too scared, and he knew what the consequences could be! Sadly, David experienced seeing other homeless people, kids and adults, who were in desperate situations, whether suffering from mental illness, addiction or the affliction of basically being runaways, which can lead to all of the former, not to mention prostitution.

At one point, a wealthy couple from America offered to take him in, but David politely declined. In facing the truth, David said "No thank you" because he was too proud. Almost immediately, he regretted it. Yet, little did he know...there was an avenue forthcoming that would lead to David's future security and well being.

David was about to learn about "Job Center"! This was a government owned job placement center that provided work opportunities for those looking for jobs. In optimistically entering this new possibility, David was more than obliged that in just one day, after fulfilling the application requirements, he was given the card for an interview the next day!

The interview was held at one of the hotels owned by the Trust House Forte Group, the company that owns many luxury hotels in London.

To David's exuberance, he was immediately hired! He was given a regular room at one of their 5 star hotels! Full room and board, plus all meals and hotel entertainment at no cost.

After three days of settling into this happy, lovely and very secure habitat, David ventured into his newfound employment at the hotel. He started out as a porter. (Gradually, he was trained in all of the hotel departments and emerged as top employee in each capacity during his seven year "reign", conclusively leading to designation as the hotel restaurant manager.)

While fulfilled in having this new job position, he recollected that at that time, his two biggest dreams were to be a singer and a hotel manager. So, along side of the Trust House Forte career, David took up singing lessons with Arnold Rosendale. (One of his clients was Blondie, and he told David that he could be the next superstar.) Thus, on one of the train rides back from Arnold's training, David started crying, because he knew he could not afford to continue on with these lessons. So, David made the decision try to earn more money in business along with his hotel career. He also heard the words of his father, Elvis in his mind… to live his life and sing later…This was something he had told David as a kid on the phone.

At age of 17, David also applied to join the Air Force, but he was rejected on medical grounds. Thus, he continued with his hotel vocation and business efforts.

Right off the bat, David made lots of friends who also worked at the prestigious hotel. In Elaine's musing nostalgia, she engagingly summons up David's affectionate recollection of Antonio. Out of all the interesting and diverse friendships David enjoyed, there was something most unique about Antonio! An Italian, Antonio was not only intelligent but funny and entertaining. He had an automatic charisma and romantic quality about him. He and David developed a fast fellowship!

A group of about eight to ten hotel comrades spent many great times on days off going to wine bars in town. It was a good group! Everybody looked after each other… big time! Elaine has a poignant memory, during these outings, when David was asked, "Are you going to go see your mom?" And, in David's deep thoughts, going back to the time at Boyle's Court when he was strongly told not to ever return home, he answered somberly that he did not think that that was a good idea at that point in time.

On one unforgettable evening, David was in Antonio's car with him when he was speeding. A female cop pulled him over. In pulling off his crazy, creative deliverance, Antonio threw his arms up in the air, speaking only in Italian and bluffing that he could not understand a word that was spoken! Rather than fiddling with the complications of this, the cop let Antonio go but warned him about being more careful down the road!!!

David and Antonio cultivated a fun time, about twice a week, going to late night pool bars/halls. This was a whole new scene for David! It was also the first time David saw Antonio in different "shoes", from playing a simple hotel kitchen dishwasher to playing a skilled pool player! And, it was perplexing for David to see this new found friend who seemingly earned much needed income from a simple job to having a whole bunch of money to play with!

It was immediately obvious that Antonio was a very brilliant champion "Player of Pool"! He was so good that most people wouldn't get a second shot when they played him. Antonio had a strategy…a very sneaky strategy…and clever indeed! He would typically start out the game pretending to play badly as the players plopped down ten to twenty pounds. Then Antonio would challenge his opponents with a 500 pound gamble. Laughingly, thinking they had it made, the other players met the challenge! Inevitably, Antonio turned on his real power game and won hands down. Gathering his money, he and David would leave rapidly and make the grand escape.

On the first time this wild flight occurred, as Antonio was attending David down the fast road to "disappearance", David suddenly "caught on" and said, "Oh my God, You're a pool hustler!" Antonio's quick response was "Just keep running!!!!"

David ended up going a few more times to other pool places with Antonio, but he steadily deciphered that it was best for him to shy away from Antonio. David felt that Antonio was a pool shark gangster!

Antonio soon left his job at the hotel. In saying "Goodbye", Antonio said that he wanted to stay in touch with David. David strongly felt that that proposition would be too precarious. Notwithstanding, David said, "Okay, I love you!"

David did not hear from Antonio for about a year. Then one day, David was walking down the street, and he saw Antonio. He was very pleased to see him again! David told him that he was doing very well at the hotel. Antonio said, "You should come and work for me!" David asked him, "What do you do?" Antonio explained that with the money he gained from his pool winnings, he had bought a house and that this house was where he was operating a prostitution and drug ring. David politely refused.

In retrospect, no matter what, David's time with Antonio was no doubt exciting! Antonio wined and dined David and bought him all kinds of things! But what stood out the most in David's mind was that, through it all, Antonio always protected him! Yet, most importantly, David ascertained that all the wild fun and exhilaration of running down the street with him to avoid getting caught or killed was not worth the risk of death!!!

Also, in overview, Elaine, as David, devotedly remembers the good, good fun with Antonio! They definitely developed a bond...a bond that Elaine still believes is unbreakable to this day!

A New Path Awaits

Since David was now living in the 5 Star employment way, he wanted to be able to enjoy the extra luxuries that others had, whether it was finer clothes shopping, finer dining or just finer living! So, on the side, David pursued other jobs!

Among these pursuits were selling horse racing gambling memberships and encyclopedia memberships. What turned out to be one of the funniest business things that he tried was to sell jewelry on the streets of London. The whole concept was to pretend that the jewelry was stolen in order to create a bigger interest to buy it. But David used to buy the goods from a wholesale company. The only illegal part was that he never had a street trader's license to sell it. So, when a policeman came along, he used to run off. One time, he ran into a department store bathroom and dropped the merchandise all over the bathroom floor. Security thought that he stole it from inside the store. It took David three hours of explaining before they let him go. This ended David's street trading career.

His next endeavor was to sell whole life insurance through Trident Life.

David demonstrated a good track record in selling insurance, and his manager wanted him to work full time. David could not do that, and since he had a new opportunity in the offing, he quit the insurance sales. When he later ran into his former insurance boss on the street, the irate boss smacked him in the face, saying "You could have made a million! You wasted your life!"

So, the big part time job in the folds was being a private investigative detective! This suited David well. He and a partner were appointed various assignments making calls. The duo was typically made up of a "good guy" officer and a "bad guy" officer. David was proclaimed the good guy!

A particularly unforgettable call occurred when the good guy and the bad guy went to the business office of a man, the manager of the business, who was involved in doing check fraud. Upon arriving at the office, they met the secretary, showed their identification and insisted on seeing the manager. Scared, she took them right to his office where David and his partner interrogated him and presented their case. Terrified and truthful, the manager wrote them a check for the fraud amount.

As the two detectives left the office, David turned to his cohort and said, "What's the name of this company?" In hearing the name, David flatly stated, "That's the company upstairs!!!"

They promptly went back into the office and gave the check back to the manager, apologizing but saying to be prepared to issue a new check to the other detectives that are handling this case! Meanwhile, as the detectives moved on to the upper level, it became apparent that the guy up there figured out that they were coming. It was obvious that he had quickly stripped his office of pertinent paperwork and had taken off down the fire escape!

In automatic retrospect, David and his partner, embarrassingly but also hilariously apprehended the fact that they had just received a confession of crime without any authorization!

So, in David's continual effort to make a fortune, he also sold Dolphin showers and Kirby vacuum cleaners. He also tackled being a plumber, which lasted only one day…after carrying a full tool box to an older lady's house to fix her washing machine. She was so thankful that David did not charge her since David knew that she was short on money. Little did she know that David had no car and that he had to carry his toolbox two miles to the train station! It was pouring down rain, and the toolbox was extremely heavy. Unable to cope with the toolbox for more than a quarter of a mile, he left the box on the side of the road…and that ended David's plumbing career.

This situation was kind of the same with selling Dolphin showers. On the day of one of his appointments, it was also raining really hard. After calling his customer, he agreed to pick David up at the train station. When they got back to his home, David was sitting there with his wife, and the man asked, "So, tell me about the showers!" David responded, "Sir, this is my first day, and I have absolutely no idea about these showers, other than the fact that this expensive one is the best one in the world for two thousand five hundred pounds." He replied, "Sign me up! I'll take one!" He then drove David back to the train station. David considered this a miracle from God.

One of the last things that David ended up selling was funeral lots. He was placed with this big religious black guy to train him. He set out driving his car like a maniac with his bible on the dashboard and David in the passenger seat holding on for dear life without any seatbelts! David said "You're going to kill us!" But he just sped down the street laughing and shouting out, "We're in God's hands, Son, we are in God's hands!'

David became so depressed with this morbid job that his sales approach became very direct. He remembers interviewing a military guy, who asked David why he should buy a burial plot from him when he had one available as a vet. David looked at him straight in the eyes and said, "If you want to rot away waiting for them to bury you, then that's fine. But, if you die tomorrow, we can bury you the next day!" They both laughed their heads off! And, he did buy a plot from David, and David quit the job the next day!

David had the pleasure of meeting and dating several girls during his employment and extent at the hotel. One particular girl, Elaine manifested to play a vital part of David's life. He met her at one of the hotel employee's parties. David asked her to dance, and they got along like magic! They fell in love and dated while at the hotel. On their days off, David luxuriated in going with her to her mother's home in Manchester where Elaine's sister lived as well.

There came a point when Elaine's family chose to move back to South Africa. (Her mom and dad had moved there in their early marriage when he was offered a job in that area. After Elaine's dad died in a car crash, her mum moved back to her original home in Manchester.) Just two weeks before this declaration, David and Elaine had become engaged.

In kind assertion, Elaine's mum asked David to venture back with them. In extremely difficult pondering, David decided to say "No". This resolution was trying and painful. But in reckoning with the concrete thought of transitioning his life to this other country, he dug into his soul to re-find the wish that he had stored away and longed for…to exist in America!

The night before the departure from London to Manchester in preparing for Elaine and her family's move, David and Elaine spent a wonderful, yet bittersweet private time together at another hotel in London. The next day, in a scene like "déjà vu" from his relationship with Linda, only in the reverse, David and Elaine sadly held on to each other for the last time at the train station…both crying so much that it seemed to never stop. After Elaine left, David went through a really hard time. He wished that he had gone!

Not long afterwards, David made an important determination. He resolved that he was tired of and not comfortable with his name as David Mower. In finding a lawyer, he changed his name to David Daniel Boden. He fondly chose Boden as his last name in honor of Elaine, as that was her last name. He still loved her very much, and he wanted to carry that name in his heart.

New Venture, New Romance

During David's prosperous vocation with the Trust House Forte Group, he always had a strong desire to start his own business. He wanted to initiate a mortgage brokerage, but he needed a way to sign up the clients for his mortgage products. So, he thought it would be a beneficial idea to offer free advice on which mortgage product would best benefit the client under their circumstances. In successfully satisfying the client's needs, he would receive a commission from the company to which he referred them.

This dream came to beautiful fruition during the last year of David's position with the hotel, from the summer of 1983 to the summer of 1984. He was eagerly looking around for a convenient space/small office to conduct this new business. David discovered in a newspaper ad that a person who owned a building on Grays Inn Road was seeking tenants to rent offices. In a subsequent interview with this person, the owner told David, "You couldn't afford an office here. But I will give you some advice: All money is created from nothing. And when you learn how to do that, you will be successful."

He then went on to say that he wanted to help David because he saw potential in him, and he was curious to see how far David could go with his endeavor. Thus, he told David that he was allowing him to use his office address for mail only, and also his secretary for any incoming phone messages. He also added David's company name, "David Boden & Company" to his company's directory.

David's business concept proved to be quite successful. This was the world's first mortgage advisory service. It became a model of its kind and was written up in the London Standard newspaper in 1984 as one of the best innovative business ideas at that time. (Eventually, it was copied, and now is utilized all over the world.)

Back on duty at the hotel, one evening while David was helping out at the reception desk, a young, gorgeous lady approached the counter to check in to the hotel. Her name was Diane, and she was on a two week "holiday" in London, having come over to England from the USA. It did not take long for David and Diane to strike up an amiable conversation.

A few days later, David took her out for a drink. (She lived in Virginia Beach, Virginia, USA with her family and was a professional model. Diane had come to London on assignment for a couple of modeling bookings and also to visit some distant relatives there.) This date was the first of many to follow.

No time lost before David's buddies at the hotel jumped on him with "Stay away from her! She's a super model and way too pretty!", implying that only trouble could lie ahead… No possible trouble in David's mind. He and Diane developed an intimate time together.

In a loving mesmerizing moment, Diane said the magic words. She loved him. And he loved her as well. Then she asked, "What are your plans for the future? David quickly replied, "Funny you should say that, as I have always felt that I needed to be in America and always had the desire to go!!!" He told her that he had been saving up with the goal of going within a year. Diane inquired, "How would you like to go back to Virginia with me?" It certainly incited his mind and heart, as David for so long had never let go of his overwhelmingly aching feeling to move to America!

Suddenly feeling that everything was happening at once and that he was being immediately and ultimately tested, David was called on to report for an important meeting with a large financial company in London, . It was apparent that they were impressed with the article in the "London Standard" about David's business changing concept that showed so much promise.

The company offered to buy him out and have David work with them, giving him a salary and 10% of the company. David firmly declined. The company kept after him, saying that this was a one of a kind offer with a big future. But David had his mind made up. He ended up selling his unparalleled idea to the company for a cash sum. No doubt, David had his eyes set on moving to America. It is important to note here that this declaration was not based on Diane's invitation for David to move with her to the states, but much more on David's longtime and ongoing eagerness to go to America.

Oceans Away To USA

Leaps and bounds! The big journey to the States became an actuality! In February of 1984, David and Diane arrived in Washington DC and then on to Norfolk, Virginia. As Elaine recalls, this whole bracing expedition brought on David's feelings of being excited and yet scared. A whole new world lay before him with his new fiancée, but the unknown was a big question mark, and David knew all too well what that meant!

Diane's parents picked them up at the airport. Diane's mom promptly sensed David's shyness and uneasiness, and she made an extra point of giving him a huge welcoming hug! After going out for a pleasant dinner, they dropped anchor at Diane's family home.

Diane's mom, Valerie was originally from England. Diane was born in New Zealand. Her real dad, Bill, divorced from Valerie, was from England as well and living in Chicago. Valerie's husband, Tony, Diane's step dad, was from Cuba.

They lived in their home with shared children. There were Diane, Minnie Anne and Phillip, offspring of Valerie and Bill. And, there were also Carter and Nancy, kids of Valerie and Tony.

David soon realized that Tony was a staunch, tough and macho guy, but he also had a fun loving and playful side! David and he got along really well from the start. After a while, they discovered many things to do together, whether it was deer hunting in the mountains, taking the boat out and water skiing or spending time on the beach.

When Diane discovered that she was pregnant, the parents insisted that the two get married. On June 29th, 1984, the family hosted a resplendent Victorian style wedding on the beach…Ocean View Beach. It was a thoroughly delightful ceremony and gathering amongst friends and family with live music and natural ambience.

David and Diane felt happy, but they both were undergoing a certain uncertainty, as the marriage was not officially their decision. They were told to not only make their way to the altar but with a discernment of urgency. In that regard, there was the lack of a smooth and gradual flow in the relationship. There was also an uncomfortable concern within David in light of his gender situation. (Diane was originally aware of this unusual circumstance when they met in London. In understanding and lightheartedness, a couple of times, she used to dress David in women's clothes.)

In David and Diane's tenure at her family home for several months before the baby was born, there was a peculiar combination of happy and fun times, with Tony treating to family dinners on the town and sporting outings, to disturbing times on the home front, when behind the scenes, Tony was occasionally hitting his wife and/or abusing her son, Phillip.

Tony, on the other hand, never hurt his own kids, Carter and Nancy. In fact…just the opposite! He stood up for his own blood, and he could use his abusive power to defend them however and whenever need be!

In view of that, one time, someone stole Carter's bike. Tony knew exactly who it was! In furious retaliation, Tony grabbed David and told him to get in the truck. They drove four doors down to the "guilty" neighbor's house. As they approached the front door and knocked, Tony implored David to stand directly behind him! As soon as the dad opened the door, Tony blurted out, "Your son stole my son's bike! Put it in the back of my truck!" With that, the man declared, "It's not your bike anymore! It's my son's bike, and it will stay on our property!" No second went by before Tony pulled out two guns, one in each hand and placed them on either side of the guy's head... "Put the bike in the truck now!" The bike was promptly placed in the truck, and as Tony got in the truck to leave with David, David pronounced, "Don't make me come back!!!"

In contemplation, Elaine, from David's point of view, discerns that this family that he was then living with and a part of, was an outline of abuse, struggles, love, protection, power, murder, success, failure and fun! Lots of stuff!!! And, also in retrospect, Elaine comments that he, in David's shoes, was never hurt or mishandled at all by Tony. He just had the misfortune of one time unhappily watching Tony hit Valerie. And, subsequently, David always had a continuing sense of being scared in knowing what Tony was capable of doing and in anticipation of what might happen.

(To fill in the whole picture, it was years later that Phillip was arrested and charged with the murder of a guy that he had been out with at the pub before going back to his home. He was sentenced to 18 years in prison, and after release, he still got into more trouble, putting him back in prison. Phillip definitely had violent tendencies, and in the original courtroom, he admitted to saying that he had repeatedly been abused by his stepfather, Tony.)

It became apparent that even though Tony could be a fun-loving and engaging guy, he definitely had a downside, oppressive element to him. It was most obvious when there was an outward verbal embattlement between him and either Minnie or Diane. It usually followed a situation when Tony would insult one of them, and they would be "fighting" back, in defending themselves.

Unheeding all of that, there developed a growing personal and professional bond between David and Tony. Tony owned a car repair garage, and David helped him out at the garage for two years doing multiple tasks before David's immigration status became confirmed.

On New Year's Eve, December 31, 1984 David and Diane's gorgeous baby girl, Bridgette was born. Elaine recalls that it was the most beautiful day of David's life. He stood by her during the whole birth process, and it was an amazing and momentous celebration! The parents, now a threesome family, had moved to a condo within a half mile from Diane's folks.

Full Steam Ahead

All along from the very beginning of Diane and David being home in Virginia, Tony unquestionably went out of his way to support and encourage David! David had originally applied for his green card, the permanent resident alien card, for proof of residency and the ability to find employment. The process takes two years to complete, but after a year and a half, David was eligible to receive his work permit card, and then he was able to pursue business opportunities. Up until then, David continued to do various odd jobs for Tony in his car repair business. Once free to pursue employment, David went "hog wild" finding all kinds of vocations. Meanwhile, Tony had a driving fascination for the real estate business! He bought training books to help educate him in the field and shared them with David. That became an ongoing mutual interest for both of them, and while David was working many different positions, he was regularly reading and studying all the aspects of real estate.

Early on, before the job activities kicked in, David set off on a "gold rush" including Valerie, his mother-in-law, in seeking good finds to sell at the flea markets. They literally plunged into trash cans selecting "goodies" which they took to the market and actually made some money here and there.

In one incident, David and Valerie thought they had hit the gold mine!!!...a huge computer with all of its parts. As they were in the big process of pulling this "baby" out and into the station wagon, the home owner turned the front house lights on. With that, David and Valerie astonishingly and quickly hid behind the bins. Standing in his doorway, the home owner saw something going on! At this point, David popped out from his vantage point and said, "Can we have this computer?" The resident says back, "Sure, fine, you can take it!"

Upon taking this "treasure" back home and in the process of taking it out of the vehicle and placing it in the driveway, all of the metal sides fell off and came crashing down! In leaving it there, they went inside to have tea and biscuits, discussing how in the next day, they would put the pieces back together and sell it to a computer dealer!

Next day at the computer dealer's store, the owner informed them that it was an old navy computer and that it was worthless. David looked at Valerie, and Valerie looked at David and they both said, "Let's get out of here!"

The next enterprise adventure panned out to be a wild flop! David bought a magazine which listed business opportunities and saw an ad for selling space pets with the lure of making 100 to 300 dollars a day! He ordered a sample for $25.00. When the box arrived, it felt awfully light as if it was empty! Then the infamous space pet popped out! He was nothing more than a blue mylar balloon with big eyes and legs dangling down! "Oh well", thought David, "I'll give it a try!" So, he ordered a few more. Meanwhile, he left the one "pet" in the house to float around…which it did, very freely roaming all over, down the hallway and up the stairs! While sleeping in the middle of the night,

David was not just jolted but terrified when the space pet grazed across his head in bed!

As David ventured into trying to make sales with this crazy item, he soon discovered that nobody was interested. Nevertheless, he took his space pets to the local flea markets, setting the price at $5.99 per pet, which was way too high! The poor pets did not attract anybody anyway. No draw! Definitely, as Elaine looks back on this mad endeavor of David's, it became one of the hysterically historic business efforts that did not work too well! And yet, another lesson to be learned.

Importantly, throughout this period of "professional discovery", David was persistently looking for ideas and possibilities to make an income to help support his daughter, Bridgette. (At the same time, he was religiously doing the courses to educate himself in real estate!) It was quite obvious that he never let up in pursuing opportunities! One vocation came about, one after the other, from selling encyclopedias, vinyl siding and family photo albums door to door, to doing liquid roof repair and working at a Cadillac car dealership. (This latter job ended abruptly when David took the potential client on a test drive which progressed to a day long stay at the beach!)

Then, David landed a nice job with ITT Technical Institute in Norfolk as a fulltime student recruiter. This turned out to be a year stint before David came upon new developments:

A bartending school! There it was, just sitting, wanting to be bought! No money down! The whole place, all equipment included, just waiting for a new owner. All David had to do was find a teacher, which he did.

For six months, the school went well…until one day, the bottom fell out! A man walked in, uninvited, sat down and stated that he owned everything! The person he had sold the business to owed him the money! He showed David the documentation, and he also showed him a knife. They got into a verbal fight. The guy threatened David, and David wanted to retaliate the threat when he realized that he should be cautious! He told David, "You have 24 hours to make up your mind. I can make you disappear, and I will."

Within that time period, David, in reviewing the paperwork, realized that the guy that "sold" David the school did, in fact, still owe the money for it. David called him, left him a message, left the keys on the desk and walked out!

After taking part in temporary assignments as receptionist at two hotels, employment then came calling again for David as a student recruiter. This time it was at the Culinary School of Washington DC. After a year of fulfilling that designation, David spent three months in Georgetown selling dating memberships. He set up appointments for clients to "show off" their profiles on video for date seekers. This was not an occupation that he liked to occupy! In recollection, an amusing adulation occurred when David asked a female applicant, "What kind of man are you looking for?" She said, "One like you!"

A Good Sign

David proceeded back to Virginia Beach where he landed a career changing engagement that finally lucratively gave him the steady cash flow that he wanted and needed to back him as he studied and built a knowledge of the real estate industry:

It all started with an ad that captured David's attention about making from $200 to $500 a week selling signs to businesses. It involved all kinds of signs from "Open" signs to "Hour" signs to giant signs and everything in between! Under his own "Boden Sign Company", he launched into a fruitful enterprise that carried him through five years of prosperous sign selling from Virginia to Florida!

In the interim, David and his father-in-law, Tony were preparing themselves to propel into the real estate field by absorbing all that they had set out to learn about the program. About two and a half years into David's gainful sign business, he and Tony started out by buying twenty houses, some of which they fixed up, and then renting them out. This turned out to be a huge headache as far as managing them and not making much money! Plus, the houses were not appreciating! Thus, they decided to sell. So, the next effort was to jointly buy apartment complexes. They brought in Tony's friend, Max on this collaboration making for a three way investment conjointly. Disappointingly, this venture presented itself with the same worthless issues resulting in not only more headaches but a migraine!

In realignment, Max went into the insurance business, and Tony went back to running his car repair operation. It was at this junction that David pulled forward the memorable statement that was made to him back in London by the mentor who had taken him under his wing and given him office space for his innovative mortgage advisory service. His impactful words were, "In order to make something, you have to create from nothing!" So, David plunged into trying to figure out how to apply this to real estate!

He bought the books that Donald Trump released. David soon realized that in order to make money in real estate, you cannot rely on the markets…You have to make money when you buy real estate, not when you sell! Subsequently, David learned how to negotiate real estate very cheaply. He designed a program to do just that, and it worked! David found himself with a program that could potentially make him $5,000 to $30,000 a month and eventually even put him in competition with Donald!

David's first attempt wound up buying even bigger, alongside Donald Trump, for the Dominion Bank Building in downtown Norfolk on the water. Trump won the deal, and David missed out on a 20 million dollar profit. But, with this eye opening experience, David learned, hard-core, how Donald did it, and he knew he could do it too!!

Elaine, as David, flamingly recalls the shining event in celebrating this real estate victory! Donald came sailing into the harbor on his white yacht. David was overwhelmingly hypnotized by the proceedings and remembers saying to a friend, "I could have done it!!!? David continued to work on his idea, in hopes to make real deals come true for himself.

Domestically, David and Diane were experiencing marital problems, which started a year after David had been working with ITT. The couple became separated in September of 1987. David agreed with Diane on joint custody of Bridgette at the time, and Bridgette became a "traveler" back and forth between her mom and dad. Soon, David moved in with his friend, Max and his wife, Heidi in Virginia Beach. David held the fort down in taking care of his daughter during her visits. Due to Diane's erratic behavior in foolishly playing around, David filed for full custody of Bridgette as the divorce filing came into place. A long custody battle ensued which David ultimately won.

The Saddest Sorrow

Around this time, after the divorce, David met Jackie. She owned a house in Keyser, West Virginia and another home in Virginia Beach, and they traveled to and from each place. It was at this period in time that David started to think seriously about his mother again. He always naturally thought about her, but time kept moving forward, and David simply did not have the funds to go and see her. All of David's money went into fighting for custody of his daughter, Bridgette. In eventually saving up the funds to go on this important visit, he made happy plans to go and visit his mum. He spoke about this forthcoming plan with Jackie, and in accommodating his busy work schedule, he planned an agenda to fly and see her in Taunton, Somerset in six weeks.

It was late 1993, and David's mum was heavy on his mind a lot, and he missed her tremendously. What he did not realize was that Dora, his sister had hired a detective to find him. He had not seen his sister since he was 13 years old. He received a telegram from her asking for David to call her immediately! He called her frantically and asked her, "Is everybody okay, and how is Mum doing?" She said, "Oh, no, no everything is fine. The reason I sent you the telegram is that Mum wants to urgently see you! There's something that she wants to tell you, but she won't tell me what it is!"

David responded, "It's funny you should telegraph me, as I had just made plans to fly and see her." Dora answered back, saying that there was no rush. She had just gone to see her in the day hospital where she stayed sometimes, and she imperatively made it known again that his mum wanted to see him and tell him something! Upon learning this, David was so happy that he was on his way to see her and to finally learn what it was that she wanted to tell him after all these years!

About two weeks before David launched on his highly anticipated trip to be with his mum, he received a call from Dora, stating that Mildred, his mum had just died. He immediately said to Dora, "You told me that she was fine! What happened?" Dora replied, "She died of a heart attack due to the doctor's prescribing the wrong medication." She was found slumped over in her chair while watching television at the hospital, where she used to go as part of her treatment. When David asked Dora about how she actually died, she reacted with the fact that the doctors marked the death as unknown.

Later on, Dora told David that she had really died of a broken heart because she did not get to see her child. David figured out that that could not be true because he was on his way to see her, and she was pleased with that and looking so forward to the visit! It was devastating enough for David to lose his mum, but what deeply overwhelmed him was that whatever she wanted to tell him had just died along with her.

In looking back now, the mysterious circumstances surrounding David's mother's death mirror the enigmatic circumstances of his father, Elvis Presley's death...The similar thread determining causes of truth between wrongful drug application/drug overdose and a massive broken heart...

On the Brink, Twice Over

After two years of living with Max and Heidi, David moved on down the road with friend, Jackie. Not long after this move, as David was continuing to persevere with his signs and real estate endeavors, driving up and down from Virginia to Georgia to Florida and back, David suddenly developed what turned out to be a major infection. It was affecting both of his lungs and his heart, and Elaine strongly remembers herself, as David, close to dying before the much needed, careful diagnosis. He was under physical siege of a "monster" collapse, between pneumonia and sepsis. He learned that this ugly physical "attacker" was actually in the process of strangling his heart. After powerful antibiotics were prescribed, a long six month recovery was on its way. In the duration, David lost a bunch of weight.

In re-visiting the point in time when David was beginning to experience signs of suffering from this predicament, he was coughing a lot during a business drive from Virginia to Florida and back. As his condition was worsening, David, in anxiety to get home, started speeding through Georgia. (Later it became clear that Georgia was not a good state in which to speed!!)

David was pulled over by police and wound up in jail! The jail cell was very, very small and very, very crowded. In being placed on the top of a bunk bed, David, already being overwhelmed with this major setback on top of feeling miserable, was extremely uncomfortable! He could hardly move in this squeezed spot, not to mention, the fact that there was a radio playing loudly, non stop, all during the night!

As if that wasn't enough, the next morning, David was taken out and put in to another jail cell, where there was a big guy in the same cell, whom David quickly realized was a "psycho".

Thankfully, about fifteen minutes later, David was brought out and told to sit down at a wooden table. While sitting there, he noticed, as looking out the window, that there were several inmates in the process of cutting grass. It brought back to mind what other cell members said to him when he first arrived: "Oh, so, you're another "Highway 95-er"?

It became quite apparent that these other highway "victims" had also been taken off the motorway. But because they could not pay their fines, they were forced to do hard labor and stay in jail for at least six months.

As David watched these guys outside doing the yard work, one of the policemen, chewing his gum like crazy, walked over to the table where David was sitting, sat down and started mechanically and tediously filling out paperwork in front of him. Then when all "was said and done" in his proposed finality, he suddenly reached over to another nearby table and pulled out, what is now known as an old fashioned manual credit card machine. He looked at David, square in the eye, and proclaimed, "That'll be $957.00, and we take Master Card, Visa or cash, but no checks! David paid with his debit card.

After David obtained his receipt, the policeman drove him back to the motorway to his car. He said to David, "You can go now." David's reaction was, "How do I know that you're not 'gonna stop me again, as I'm still in Georgia???!!!"…The officer's quick response was, "If I was you, I'd drive as fast as you can to the state line!"

(Several months later, in the national news media, there was a story, warning people in regards to driving through Georgia, as police were snatching people/tourists in cars off the highway and throwing them in jail.)

David returned to Virginia Beach for an additional year with Jackie and continued his travels with the sign business, up and down from Virginia to Florida. When Jackie heard from her brother that he was moving to Elizabeth City, North Carolina, she and David decided to move along there too. So, off they went to Elizabeth City! And, they ended up renting a trailer in the same park as her brother, about five trailers away.

David and Jackie really, really enjoyed every minute of living in the trailer park, complete with dirt roads and everything "country"! By the end of about a year in being there, while David was still selling signs all over North Carolina, Jackie's brother decided to move back to California. In that process, her brother's dog, a rottweiler, named Buffy was left with David and Jackie. The dog was wild and uncontrollable! Therefore David, in a hard decision, as he adored this dog, found a home for him. With much despair, David found out a few weeks later that Buffy had been run over by a car, dying instantly. This sorrowful happening was so distressing for David that he could not bear to stay in this same environment.

Thus, David and Jackie moved down to Fort Meyers, Florida. (Prior to the move, it was evident that Jackie was becoming very tired, more and more, and very weak. She was also beginning to lose weight.) When David came back from his important court date regarding full custody of Bridgette in Virginia Beach, he discovered that Jackie was quite ill. She had suddenly lost a lot of weight and had a hard time moving.

After being rushed to the hospital in Fort Meyers, Jackie's diagnosis became evident. She was suffering from colon cancer. A successful surgery followed, and soon thereafter, the two of them moved back to Virginia Beach where they found an apartment. Then, once a week, for about three months, David religiously and slowly drove her to the Bethesda Military Hospital in Bethesda, Maryland, which was a four hour long journey one way and back, for Jackie's chemo treatments.

(What later became very apparent in recollection, was that, in the latter part of living in Virginia, when Jackie was experiencing these feelings of exhaustion and weakness, unknowing that there was an aggressive cancer growing inside her, there were no symptoms of pain or discomfort whatsoever.)

The final reality delivered good news with Jackie's full recovery! This was such a thankful and joyous conclusion, especially considering the fact that Jackie was on the verge of dying. On a similar pattern, though, of course, with a different story, it brought back the jolting memories of David's prior close call, on his own brink of death with his massive infection! On both notes, the fortunate results brought on a huge wave of gratitude!

From Pitiful to Plentiful

David relied on the sales of his signs for income and financial survival. After receiving Jackie's "clean bill of health", it was "on the road again" for the couple, and David was selling signs everywhere from Kissimmee to Orlando to Destin to Vero Beach. It was a life for about a month or so of going from spot to spot, living briefly in motels and barely "making ends meet".

The realization set in that Vero Beach would be a very nice locality in which to ultimately live. But, the fact of reality was that that could not be affordable by just selling signs, not to mention the circumstance that this current pattern of existing was just not the way to go.

Hence, a new horizon was about to unfold, very meek and mild, yet emboldened with the power to conquer!!!!!!!!

Along the road, half way between Destin and Vero Beach, David and Jackie came upon a "For Rent" sign. It turned out to be a kind of trailer park with lots of "sheds". They were actually primitive wooden shacks with tiny porches.

So, they moved in! David continued his signs operation, moving around the area, selling to local businesses.

In retrospect, as Elaine states, "Living in these shacks was just about as low as you can get!" Occasionally, David would "hang out" and talk with the "next door" neighbor. He was a construction worker and drove an old truck. (It became apparent later that this guy was undergoing trouble in getting custody of his children.)

One early morning, David woke up to the appearance of an ambulance and a police car outside his shed. It was sadly discovered that this guy next door had hung himself inside his shed.

About a week after this tragic occurrence, the realization that David had been facing came to a crude point. It was time to move on out of this place! As hard as David tried, he and Jackie had been suffering financially. The rent for the shed had to be paid every week, and David's rent on the shed was two weeks behind. Plus, in sheer reality, the existence there was fragile indeed! In the latter part of their time there, the winds of a storm blew two of the sheds down to the ground.

In desperation, David knew that in some way, he had to be successful in order to survive! It was either the streets or success. He had four days left to pay the next week's rent. He was sitting on the shed's little front porch having a beer and thinking… "I've got to get successful in four days, and I have 25 dollars left to my name."

This became the dramatic turning point when David remembered the impactful comment that was made to him by the banker in England, basically saying that you have to learn to create something from nothing. David immediately thought, "Oh yeah, I got that covered!" He knew, from reading and digesting Donald Trump's books, that all he had to do was to get himself out there and do a deal! David always had that real estate knowledge in the back of his mind, and now it was the time to apply it!!!!

The surge of motivation was felt out of desperation! The other powerful motivator was David's concern about his daughter, Bridgette and how badly he wanted to go and get her!!!

In his burst of enlightenment, he looked at Jackie and said, "I'm gonna get us a house in Vero Beach!" She looked back at him as if he was completely crazy!

In knowing that David could not make the last two payments of rent, and with four days left on the second week, David had a talk with the manager. (This manager pretended to be the land baron of his kingdom. He acted as a domineering landlord who knew how to keep everything tight and right. In reality, he was nothing more than "the manager of sheds", living in a trailer in the middle of a field filled with lots of shacks.)

Regardless, this "shack owner" had developed a heart on heart understanding and eventual agreement with David. He gave David and Jackie four days to leave, with the loyalty that David would make it up, "down the road", for the two weeks lost rent.

David turned those four days into a most formative and teeming engine of obstinacy and progress. In the first two days, in between selling the signs, David cruised around Vero Beach in his car with sharp focus on looking at different houses all over the area. He knew in his clear and determined mind that in order to make this real estate deal happen, the house had to be empty!

In David's quest for a house for sale, he discovered a gated community with the gates open! As he drove around the circle of homes, he noticed "the home" near the cul de sac with a "For Sale" sign. In calling the realtor, David set up an appointment for the next day!

To his wonder, David found this wooden home of 2, 500 square feet settled in this private tennis court "society" to be strikingly lovely with an open floor plan including cathedral ceilings with two fans on either side of the atrium, sky lights, three bedrooms, and two baths. There was a two car garage and a lawn sprinkler system. And, the house was EMPTY!!!

As he explored the house, in talking with the lady realtor, the humongous challenge was right there in front of David's eyes! He knew that he had no money and no way to make a down payment! He also knew that he could not afford a monthly payment on the mortgage!

In the reality of knowing that time was crucial and that there was a dire need to have a place to live, to David's delight and astonishment, he learned that the owner had no mortgage on the property! Plus, the owner preferred to have someone living in the home, rather than having it empty!

Thus, David's offer was simple: A 500 dollar deposit with the contract to be paid with check. Closing of property in 90 days. The owner to give David a first mortgage on property for 95% financing and the rest in cash. Then, David added the request to give him immediate occupancy upon acceptance of contract and keys to the house.

The next day, the "bells chimed"! David got the phone call from the realtor saying that the owner had accepted the deal!!! On that same day, the house keys were secured! David and Jackie moved in within an hour! A major celebration ensued, hallowing an amazing creative deal and the remarkable transition from the poor shack life to the environment of the rich!

Strategy for Success

Despite and in light of this incredible maneuver, the sheer reality lay starkly before David. At this potent point, it was powerfully obvious that David severely needed a quick $500 before his check to the realtor would clear. (Typically, it took within five to seven days for this earnest money deposit to occur.)

Needless to say, David busted his ass successfully selling signs like never, ever before! But, in immediacy, to play it safe, he begged the bank for an overdraft of $400 so the check would make it through. He knew he had to make $100 in a week, which he did. It all worked! But, even though David and Jackie were very happy living in this astonishing new home, David was well aware that he had to maintain this initial level of success!

So, just down the street, there was a neighborhood with hundreds of houses. They were worth between $45,000 and $65,000. Each home was typically a modest 1000 to 1200 square feet, three bedroom, two bath, stucco structure with white picket fences. It was the perfect real estate investor's dream area, and David knew that his prosperity lay right there!!! Therefore, he went home and set his mind to designing a plan for each one of these homes to be sold. He also acknowledged that he had to sell these "babies" fast!

Here's where David's knowledge and experience from his past came in handy!!! He had created his victorious mortgage advisory service in the UK. Thus, in light of that, the first thing he focused on was his ability to fix people's credit. He knew and had previously proven that many people that didn't think they could buy a home, actually could!

In kind, along these lines, David designed a classified ad that said, "3 bedroom, 2 bathroom, cute home in nice, safe neighborhood - $59,900 – good, borderline or no credit okay." He placed the ad in local newspapers, in the real estate for sale section. (David knew in full and immediate awareness that he had to have buyers as quickly as possible, as he had virtually no money and no houses for sale. He also knew that he was not looking for "fixer-uppers", as he had no funds to fix anything and no houses to fix!)

The good news was that in those days, differently from now, somebody could obtain an FHA loan with reasonable credit, and the owner of the house didn't have to own a home for any period of time before a buyer could buy a home from you. And, this is very unlike now in today's times when one has to own a home physically for ninety days before one can sell it on an FHA loan.

At this point, let's keep in mind, as Elaine now says in reliving David's life, he still did not own any other houses, besides his own…which he still had not closed on! And, he needed the money to close on it!!!

So, David went to the neighborhood with all the little houses for sale and wrote down every one of them that was for sale. Thus, he had an inventory for houses for sale, even though he did not yet own them.

Well, guess what? Phone calls started coming in madly with "We're calling on the house for sale!" And David's response/presentation was simple: "That's lovely! What I do is this...I am a consultant and an investor. I help people who normally figured that they could not buy. I assist them to become a home owner, in being able to buy a house on a regular mortgage interest rate, versus a high interest rate, when people end up in foreclosure because they could not afford high interest rate payments."

Following this, David simply asked a few questions, in determining whether these folks can buy now, in six months or in three years. He then explained that in either way, they will find out if they can buy a home now, or if not, when they will be able to buy a house in the future.

He continues, "I work closely with my friend who owns a mortgage company, and together, we assist you. The consultation is complimentary. You just pay $60.00 for three different credit reports. And then after your meeting with me, you will know your particular program. As long as you like the home you're going to buy from me, we should be able to get you into the home...Are you interested?"

Interested buyer: "Yes!!!!"

David' response: "Okay, here's what I need you to do...There are two things:

First, drive down to the house that's for sale and see if you like it, on the outside. Here is the address.

Secondly, if you do like it, come to see me and bring $60.00. (Or, if you are buying with your husband/wife, that will be $120.00.)

Thirdly, if you qualify, I will show you the inside of the house."

David made close to twenty appointments for people to come to his home and fill out applications. (On a side note, what David did not realize was that out of ten folks that came, four of them who thought they would not be eligible to buy, found out that they could!!! In addition to that, to David's surprise, the potential buyers were so excited over his program that they brought along two or three extra potential buyers!!!)

In Elaine's retrospect, with a comical look on her face, there was one evening during this overflowing process that brought unusual attention. There were so many people, waiting to fill out applications, who were lined up from the driveway to the front door of David's house, that the drug squad turned up with guns in cars and helicopters!!!...only to find out that houses were being sold, not drugs!!!

In backing up, Elaine recalls what David had to do before these prospective buyers arrived. He had to take a risk, in hopes that some of them would qualify. So, before they came, he ran out and put contracts on houses that he had already sent people to see…about 20 to start. And the deals went like this…Here is an example:

David's strategy was: "If you want to invest in houses, you don't have to go and find a "fixer-upper", because every one of these homes has already been renovated for sale at retail prices with families living in them. So, his deal with each family was: A discounted cash price for the home, a $500.00 deposit, and that deposit to be held by escrow agent who closes the deal. The balance in cash within 30 and 45 days. I also have the rights, within that period of days, to have access to the home and to inspect it."

Because David was an excellent negotiator and because he was paying cash, he managed to discount houses up to $30,000 each, and many times, the homes that he could only get a 4 to 5 thousand dollar discount on, were actually worth more than what they were trying to sell them for. Thus, along with this discount, he could increase the price of the house to the true retail price of the house and make $15,000 to $20,000 versus $4,000 to $5,000.

To re-cap, here was David with twenty contracts to buy twenty properties for cash with $5000.00 in escrow deposits that he didn't have! In reality, he had just written out checks that needed to clear! But, this was by the fact that he now controlled these properties by contract, giving him the legal right to sell them.

So, David went back home, and the next day, he called all of the buyers who qualified under the program to come and sign their contracts. He had so many qualified buyers that he sold all of his homes in one week. Each home was sold under the FHA loan program, meaning that buyers only needed 3.5% down payment. They also paid him a deposit on each home of $3000 each, meaning that herein he had $60,000 in cash.

He always asked for a higher deposit so that the buyers would not back out, as no one wants to lose a $3000 contract deposit. David only had to pay the escrow company $5000, leaving him with $55,000 in cash...AND he hadn't even closed on the houses yet!!!

This program will not work in current time because the laws on FHA loans have changed. On the humorous side, David usually would get a phone call from the sellers of the homes, asking him if he would bring a big sum of cash for them at closing. And, David always used to respond, "No, M'am, I'm going to take a nice chunk home with me!" They both laughed, with the seller thinking that he was joking!

In aftermath, with renewed understanding, inspiration and determination, David strategically cultivated his plan following the Trump method. He unrolled his own knack of buying and selling properties to perfection, which evolved into a track record of genuinely staying ahead of the game in this profession! Inevitably, David's proficient practice brought in the steady assets that made his dream come true for supporting his daughter and living a more comfortable life. Happily, he advanced to maneuvering over one thousand properties between Virginia and Florida. David's success enabled him to go out of his way and in always following his natural inclination, to buy nice homes for his family and cars for everyone! That included his daughter, his stepmom, two friends and himself.

Elaine distinctly pulls back one memory of David going to a St. Petersburg car dealership and purchasing a jeep for himself and a new white Honda Accord CRV for a friend who had cancer. He gave them over $50,000 in cash!

David went on to consult, buy and sell over a thousand homes using this strategy. Interestingly and ironically, today in time, mortgage advisors use a similar credit consulting program that David had designed in the old days back in England in 1984. As a funny side note, David had to be careful about telling investors where he bought homes, as he was so good at picking the right homes, and investors liked to follow him.

After being so prosperous with this enterprise, David consulted with other investors who were in trouble with their real estate investments. Just a simple classified ad, looking for investors who were having troubles with their properties, netted him hundreds of thousands of dollars in consulting fees.

Not long after David's lucrative success, he stood by his promise to the owner of the shacks where he and Jackie used to live, and he delivered the last two rent payments that he owed.

A New Chapter, A Winning Case

David continued selling real estate in Vero Beach for a couple of years. His daughter, Bridgette came on visits in the summer time. It eventually became time for David to move back to Virginia Beach in order to prepare for the final court date on custody of Bridgette. Soon thereafter, David made the decision to split up with Jackie. The realization was clear that he was living more of a friendship life than a relationship life with her. (Part of the issue was David's gender situation, which had always stood in the forefront of David's life.) In knowing that Jackie, who was older than David, had found a job, he felt that she would be secure.

David, hence, went on to move into a house in Newport News. Eight months down the line, he faced one of the most, if not the most, momentous and life changing occurrences of his life: The immense and emotional goal of gaining full custody of his daughter, Bridgette! David made his appearance in court in Virginia Beach.

As Elaine so strongly recalls, in David's immovable shoes, he simply told the truth! There were important facts about Diane, Bridgette's mother, that needed to come forward. Diane had been trying to use the "physical abuse" clause, which was totally false. Fact of the matter, David had been sending money and support in constantly taking care of Bridgette, as well as for Diane all of the time.

The ultimate winning result came down in final light of two salient factors: The happy photographs from the recent trip to Disney World (where David took his ex-wife, Diane and daughter, Bridgette) were presented. That was major. But, what was much, much more major was that the judge took Bridgette in to a private room, and she explained to the judge that her father had never abused her mom.

Back in session, it became obvious, through Bridgette's testimony, that she preferred to live with her father. Mother, Diane "caved in" as she herself knew that Bridgette wanted to live with David, yet still have rights to see her mom whenever she wanted to. Justifiably, David was ecstatic over the final decree, and he ardently and warmly took his daughter home with him. They stayed in Newport News for awhile, but David felt vehemently that Bridgette should continue to have a good education. (His daughter had already attended the Montessori school in Virginia Beach and had been in very decent schools throughout the whole custody battle.)

Fate stepped in, and David met Adele in Virginia Beach. There was an immediate attraction. Adele had two children, Karen and Julie. They lived in Salem, Virginia. When they met, Adele was visiting her sister in Virginia Beach. David enjoyed spending visits with Adele at her sister's home.

Adele's daughter, Karen had been suffering with mental disorders and had tried to commit suicide. She wound up in a mental institution for suicide prevention. In David's desire for the two of them to be together but also for Bridgette to be in a good school system, as well as for Karen to keep getting the help she needed, David bought a home for all of them that was overlooking the mountains, about a mile from downtown Salem, Virginia.

The house was a gem. It "shone" with a big open floor plan that was dramatic, yet embracing warmth and comfort. The pride and joy was the dining room which had a crystal chandelier with hanging glass grapes and a gorgeous wood table. The windows had electric candles that turned on at nighttime. (People used to like driving by the home at night just to see the chandeliers!)

The new combined family got along well, except for the underlying feeling that Bridgette had about her dad having "other daughters". The best news was that Bridgette was able to go to a fine school, the Cave Springs high school, which was the answer to David's prayer for her, and that Karen was still very secure at the institution.

The first agenda in David's caring mind was to make sure that all the kids were safe and getting a good education and/or all the help that they needed. Several months after the move, David made the decision, with Adele's one hundred percent approval, to keep Karen out of the institution and bring her home! As time was told, it could not have been a better decision, as thankfully, David managed to not only help Karen recover but to help her become a very happy child and also do well in school.

In Elaine's affectionate and powerful retrospection of what she feels and knows in David's helping Karen to turn herself around was the knowledge of telling her that he loved her and that she had two choices: If she continued to try to kill herself and should ever succeed…then she wouldn't be with David and Adele anymore, and they would drastically miss her! Or, if she might become institutionalized again, she could become so bad mentally that the hospital may not let David take her home anymore…plus the fact that she might be put on drugs which could be damaging, not to mention make her unaware of who she was!

Undoubtedly and happily, this made a shocking impression on Karen, and thankfully, in due process, her life took a huge change of course for the better!

Fun Times Coming

Moving to Salem and being able to have his daughter, Bridgette go to a good school was a tremendous relief for David! Salem is right next to Roanoke, Virginia in a valley overlooking four states. As one comes over the mountain into the valley at night time, the Roanoke Star shines ever so brightly over the Blue Ridge Mountains! The city of Salem was clean, the people were friendly, and it proved to be a wonderful place to live and raise a family! Also, David's satisfaction of being with Adele and Bridgette and his two adopted kids in a nice, new beautiful home looking down on the mountains could not have been more refreshing. This habitat, as Elaine serenely recalls in memories as David "gave the children, Adele and me a happy, stable home."

In remembering the good times at the home on Saddle Drive in Salem, it was always a pleasant sensation, every now and then when David drove to work, to have Adele and the three kids follow him in the other car until they reached the mountain pass to leave town. And, as David drove over the mountain pass, the kids would throw their arms out the car window, waving them up and down like an airplane! As Elaine immensely relives these exhilarating moments, as David, she recounts, "It was an awesome feeling and a great motivator to do well for our family!"

In more nostalgic moments, every Friday, the joined kin went out together as a "family", and they chose to either eat at a Japanese restaurant or to have macaroni and cheese at another place. Basically, they spent fun times, whether it was shopping in the mall, or visiting friends and families in their homes for barbecues and parties.

Most memorably, they often, about twice a week, drove up at night to the Roanoke Star. They all would habitually walk to the edge over the mountain and pray, making wishes to the Star. These special moments brought pure serenity.

David potently felt that these cherished episodes reflected the first time that he had been really happy since the death of Elvis in 1977. Naturally and of course, one of the happiest, if not the happiest occasion occurred when Bridgette was born and carried forward in the ultimate joy of raising her.

The salient fact of the matter was that down deep inside, David was still very lost. But, he had learned to push it aside, as well as dealing with his gender issue. As Elaine describes so well, in reenacting David's life, "The best way to explain the 'lost' feeling is in two parts:

Firstly, I had a family that I loved with Adele, Bridgette and her two kids, but I didn't have the foundation of what most people have, in knowing who their parents are. As a child, even though I thought I knew who my dad was, my heart and soul were trying to lead me to who I was, but my brain was confused.

Secondly, there was the gender thing. This was a nice benefit for everybody, except Adele, because I was a brilliant mother with all of the "mom" instincts, yet still trying to be an excellent father. In dealing with my confusion in my role as a dad, even though successful, I had to learn about and embellish on being a man, because I had no clue as to how to be a man properly. I knew David was truly a woman but trying to be a man. Being a woman was natural. Being a man was not.

In both of these worlds, I had a great understanding of people! I also had a 'second seeing eye', good instincts and perfect gut and spiritual feelings.

I was very good at 'reading' people, analyzing, recognizing, foreseeing and avoiding dangers. I was fortunately able to always keep the children safe and on track with their schooling. We had a reward system, as many do. When the kids did well in school, we used to prop the results on the refrigerator. Bridgette was good in school, but she had to be pushed a little harder in order to achieve better results.

Bridgette did not really like the other two children, as she did not want to share her father with them. However, I did feel it was good that she did share me because, in that way, she could ultimately be more independent in the future, and as far as within herself, be loving and giving. (Bridgette ended up graduating, and I was very proud of her! Everything worked and came into place, and my daughter became a very fine and well rounded young lady.)"

In continuation of the good times with the newly founded family of David and Adele and their children, David was excited to have Karen and Julie in his life. Even though Karen had some problems, as previously divulged, David could see in her a happy, bouncy, intelligent and talented young lady! Julie, on the other hand, was quiet and reserved. She did her duties methodically, including homework, chores, and keeping her room clean and tidy. These factors worried David a little bit, as she was often very quiet. However, after a while in knowing her, David realized that because of this characteristic, she gained satisfaction in life. Plus, Julie still did all of the family fun things!

Once Karen became stable and happy, and no longer having the desire to kill herself, the family could start living a normal life.

When Bridgette got her driver's license, everybody in the family was so happy for her, and they all went out for dinner to celebrate! The kids fancied their favorite macaroni and cheese at their chosen restaurant.

The family bunch had many sporting and relaxing times, such as parties at their home, barbecues, pinata events, etc. But mainly, it was the thrill and comfort of being part of the family dinners, just the family itself, at home under their crystal chandelier with hanging grapes. They also often visited Adele's parents at their house close by and sometimes also went to visit Adele's sister in Virginia Beach.

(On one of these times, Karen was driving back home by herself, when she was hit by a snow storm on top of the Blue Ridge Mountains. She became stuck in the blizzard and needed desperately to be rescued. Her life was in grave danger, and many people have certainly died in storms like this. David immediately set out to rescue his daughter. Luckily, they were on the same road, and David was only a short distance from her. When David found her, she was terrified, freezing and crying. He gave her a big hug and brought her back home.)

Moving on back now to the fun and happy times, each of the kid's school life was the center of all of their attention. And, the shows and functions that took place at the school were marvelous!

One of these special events was the time when Bridgette took the stage and played the violin. (She had been enjoying her violin lessons at her school for two years!) It was indeed a proud moment for all of the family!

Julie loved to act! And, Karen loved to sing! All of the girls' performances were spellbinding. Bridgette played the violin beautifully, Karen was a rising singing star, and Julie was a wonderful actress! At times, the three sisters were in shows together. Of course, David and Adele always went to these shows, and there was always a standing ovation.

There were also other simply wonderful times as a family! And, one of the things in merriment to do was to wash the cars with hoses in the summertime and get each other wet! Anyone could hear their giddy laughter from miles away! Without question, this was a very happy family!

A Big Switch!

In due time, there were hard realities that were seething and building underneath all of the happiness. As stated earlier, Bridgette resented her two step sisters. This was not only because she did not want to share her father, but because Adele's two daughters, behind the scenes, were very conniving. While they were "playing" lovely and pleasing to David, they were nasty to Bridgette behind David's back.

In addition to this, Adele had been lying to David about many factors involving their relationship. This devastating truth was slowly but inflexibly playing out in the background of the family unit. In retrospect, it was evident that David had gone out of his way for the combined couple and offspring. He had bought a beautiful home for them. He had purchased cars, furnishings and clothes. His support, help, and assistance were always available when needed. And, of course, he was always reliable in providing an unlimited supply of money. The children had made it well through a fine education. As Elaine reassembles in her mind what David, dejected and dismayed, endured, she states "Now that her kids were stable and graduating, Adele was making other plans."

One day, David was with the kids over at Adele's mother's home, and while they were having a family barbecue, Adele turned up later, and it became obvious by her behavior that she was having an affair with her boss. (Adele was the kind of woman that was very countrified with manipulation. And she had applied this technique on many different men. She actually was appearing quite old, due to the fact that she constantly had to lie.)

As this stricken discovery began to surface in the last several months of the three-year relationship, the foremost tragedy was the fact that Adele's kids did not want to leave David. In sadness and in thinking back, Elaine admits that David, in going in on the relationship, had a strong feeling about this dysfunction on Adele's part. But he thought optimistically that he could turn everything around because of the perfect setup with the whole environment, including the home, the schooling, etc. Yet, in Elaine's words as David, "Was I an angel myself? I was no angel." In surmising, David was actually lost and was attempting to use this "perfect" family to cover up his pain of being desolate, feeling abandoned and not knowing who he was.

On the other hand, regarding this situation and in light of David's innate characteristics, being so much like his real father, Elvis… with all of his love, charisma, care and tenderness, many women wanted to date him. But, did he go ahead and date all those alluring women and have a rousing time? No! Well, Adele thought he did, as she was having multiple affairs….

Nevertheless, David was indeed re-engaging and "playing out" his own scenario on the other side of the curtain. He was doing what he did as a youngster …dressing up as a girl. He used to occasionally go out of town on his business trips, dressed as a woman. In recollection, he had been dressing up as a girl and having boyfriends as early as he could remember…Not to mention, as previously told in this story, David's mom used to dress him up for a long time until she was told to stop. David hid the fact that he wanted to be a female for all of his life. In proper perspective, David was not lost as a child. He only felt extremely misplaced. He only became lost, truly lost in 1977 when his dad, Elvis died. At that "intersection" of his life, David took a different turn to avoid the same fate as his dad.

Elaine remembers herself as David being a seventeen year old in London, dressing up as a girl in a mini skirt. He looked really hot, and men wanted to hang out with him and date him. He also had a dynamic charm as well as a loving and caring personality. His sexy, bright green eyes, big juicy lips, awesome smile and the softest skin were all "to die for"! In general, and in moving on, he was so much like a girl that he had to try really hard to be like a guy!

Also, as mentioned earlier in this writing, when he married Diane, she used to dress him as a woman, as she knew that he liked it. An important note that Elaine wants to bring out here is that David desired that all these former factors come out! He wanted people to know that he really was a girl, in his heart and soul, all of his life, rather than having people think that he was suddenly dreaming this up later on in life.

There simply was not the education or social acceptance back then for him to get help. So, he tried to be the man that everybody wanted him to be. But, in essence, he really had no idea how to be a man. And, when people ask her now, "What was it like to be a man?" She responds, "I don't honestly know."

Moving forward now, back to Adele and David and the "family", the situation was distinctively bizarre, to say the very least: Adele was having affairs and being deceptive. David was running around being a woman and feeling lost within himself. And, the kids were hating each other behind the scenes. (This unhappy dilemma had grown worse in time, as the kids were realizing that the once parental "rock" was crumbling.)

Now, because of all this mess, David knew that things would eventually come to an end. Thus, for fun and curiosity, in still trying to live out his role as a man, he sought out a dating service on the internet….David met Susan. In the meantime, Adele was still seeking another boyfriend, because she and the former one were not getting along at all. She ended up finding one. Then, one day, Bridgette was coming back from school to find that Adele had moved her new boyfriend into the house and had thrown all of David and Bridgette's stuff out of the house on the ground. Karen and Julie were totally distraught and upset, as they loved David very much, and David loved them too. Undeniably, David was emotionally demolished to see this impact on them!

However, Adele had one big problem that she did not think about…David owned the house!

Turning the Tables

Here David was, homeless, sitting in his car with his daughter. He immediately drove to a nearby apartment complex just outside of Salem in Roanoke, about a half a mile from Cave Spring High School. He rented an apartment for his daughter and himself and bought all new furniture. He enlisted Bridgette in Cave Spring High School. So, they became once again "stable" in a new location. Bridgette was actually very content with this situation, as she now had her daddy all to her own.

So much, in alleviation, came back to normal. In the mornings, David would wake up to fix Bridgette her breakfast, take her to school and then later bring her home after school. In between times, he worked on his real estate deals.

David became aware that he had to design a plan for what to do in regards to the house, to Adele and to the other two children. First of all, he investigated the guy, named Steve who was now living in the house. His conclusion was that he could possibly be dangerous. It was a fact, as Adele had told David, that he carried a gun. But, importantly, due to his contractor job, Steve did not have the way or the means to support Adele and/or the kids, not to mention, to even begin to pay the mortgage on the house... And, why would he make the payments anyway, as he did not own the house!

In the midst of this impasse, David's forthcoming decision was a long and hard one. He confronted a truly challenging resolution that pulled furiously on his heartstrings, as he struggled to bring his emotional agenda in alignment with his mentally best wisdom: David's other two daughters lived in that house, and he loved them very, very much! Yet, his own daughter, Bridgette, who was so relieved to be back with her dad, totally despised those two girls and was ever so joyful to be away from them! This was definitely one of the most soul destroying experiences that David had to face living out in his whole life.

Firstly, he needed to get the rest of his belongings and bits and pieces out of the house. And, he needed to analyze the inside of the home and also see how the girls were doing, with great respect and respectively to how safe the environment was. Also, because he still owned the house and technically lived there, he did not need a court order.

Without a doubt, this situation had all the earmarks of being a conceivable hazard. Because David was raised and trained by the Army Cadets and was brought up in a family of trained and decorated marines, they taught him how to survive! Thus, David made the big plan to go into the house and leave with mission accomplished!

He got into the house, dissected every room, retrieved a few of his things and left. As he was leaving, one of Adele's friends, Carol who was in the house, was entering the garage door to go out of the house as David was leaving the garage to go out in the street. He quickly ran to his car while she screamed, "David's here!" As they chased David down the street with weapons, he jumped into the car and spun off! Adele called the police. When the policemen later arrived at David's apartment door, in the understanding that it was David's house where this incident occurred, they simply told him not to do it again. Fortunately, David did get the information that he was seeking.

Conclusively, as time rolled along during an eight month period, it became crystal clear that Adele's boyfriend, Steve did not actually want to live there at all. And he certainly did not want to make the house payments. He could not afford them anyway! But, most significantly, he had lied to Adele and told her that he had more money than he did. His inner goal was to move her and the girls out of that house and into his own home in Winchester, Virginia. (Patsy Cline territory.)

Thus, David knew that he needed to give Adele a nudge, as there was no way that he would ever be making payments for another person living in his house, and with his children! In dealing with all of this, David's well devised plan was to wait for the foreclosure, which typically takes nine months, and then go back and buy the house back from the bank. (as foreclosure would have evicted her.)

Understandably, David abhorred doing this to Karen and Julie, but he had no choice. Adele, in her furious outrage over this plan, sued him, along with claims that he beat her up. David hired the best attorney in town and won on every account. He also got the house back! Because his daughter did not want to live there, and he did not have his other two girls with him, it was way too much of an emotional distress to even think of living in that house again. The original magic of the home was gone. Harsh reality was setting in. The home was now just a house.

David still hung onto the hope that Adele and his girls would end up moving in with him, as they were so fond of David that they even wanted to change their last name to David's name! Even though he knew so well that that would not sit well at all with his daughter, Bridgette, he fantasized that maybe the three girls would get along somehow.

Adele talked the kids into moving to the home of her boyfriend, Steve in Winchester, which they did. David was so distraught over losing his kids that he just let the home go back to the bank. Adele let him see the girls one more time before they moved. Karen was very angry with him, and when he left them, he felt, in realization, that he really screwed things up! But, he simply could not allow a man to live in his house with his newly found daughters.

The move of Adele and the girls to Steve's place in Winchester lasted for about six months. Steve consequently threw them out, and Adele and the kids ended up living with her sister in Virginia Beach. He simply could not put up with Adele's lies, and through the grapevine, David found out that Steve could not get over what Adele did to David. (And, this showed David, at the "end of the day", that he was indeed a decent man.) David still wanted so badly to get back his girls, but Bridgette put her foot down and demanded that she never wanted to see either of them again. Bridgette implored, "Can't you see what they all did to you?" David said, "Okay, I will do what you want." Of course, David adored his own daughter with all of his heart and soul, but he also held a special place in his heart for Karen and Julie.

One of David's best friends in Virginia Beach passed along the information to him that Karen was doing karaoke singing. David passed back his response, via his friend, to Karen that she had a super star voice and that she should go for her dreams of being a real singer. He also said that he hoped to one day turn on the "telly" to see daughter, Karen singing. It would be a proud day! In recognizing this, he would always have a dear spot in his heart for both Adele (and his) girls.

Old Stomping Grounds

After this overwrought saga, it was now all about digging into the new life, space and time for Bridgette and her dad in the apartment in Roanoke. As Bridgette attended high school, with one year before graduation, as stated earlier, David spent his days working real estate, taking his daughter back and forth to school and doing the usual family stuff...going out for dinner, seeing friends, and playing games, including monopoly, chess, checkers, and playing cards etc. (There was another company of David's, as well as his real estate business, that he had organized when living with Adele and the kids in Salem. He named it "T-A-Can-Co International Corporation". It was an investigative and debt collection company.)

David was also developing a relationship with his new romance, Susan, whom he had met online. She lived in Melton Mowbray of Leicestershire, England. At the time, she was an HR manager at a hotel. She had a daughter and a son from a previous marriage. She also wrote articles on the subject of human resources and business courses. She was highly recognized for her innovative talent in designing business programs to help women get back on their feet.

David arranged to go to England and meet Susan when Bridgette was basically out of school in the summer, except for taking a few summer courses. David felt good about his father/daughter session with Bridgette in regards to the upcoming two week jaunt to England. He felt confident that Bridgette would be safe, and he trusted her in her judgements surrounded by their friends in the Roanoke Valley. Boy, Oh, Boy, Mercy, Mercy, Oh, what lay ahead!!!...

David thus flew to London and took a train to Colchester to hook up with Susan, and she drove from Melton Mowbray to meet him. David had two reasons for this location, which was a neutral and mutual spot to meet: 1) To go and visit his older sister, Dora who lived in Colchester. 2) To go back to Coggeshall where he had spent his boyhood and play on the swings in the park, etc. 3) To go and see the man he had thought to be his father...Dennis.

David soon found out that he was not allowed to just go to the house. He had to put a plan together for all of that through Dora. There was nothing official or anything. It was just a matter of satisfying Dora's wishes. Also, there was the warped matter that Dennis's wife loathed David because he loved his mother.

The immensely strange thing about all of this was that he was yet again following Dora's rules, as she had kept him from Dennis and vice versa on the times when David had tried to come back and visit. And, herewith in actuality, David only got to see him one time in town for no more than one minute. And, in that meeting, David looked at a "stranger" whom he never knew and had never known. This disturbed David greatly, as he discerned...Why was he looking at a man, who was a stranger and he had no feelings or connections with him whatsoever?

The biggest quandary was that Dora had always spent a considerable amount of time keeping Dennis to her and James's selves. David still just could not figure out why he was kept out of the family and why everybody was more cold and aloof towards him. It was as if they knew something that David did not know! David had always tried so hard to give his all and to be loving and caring. But, nothing worked. It perpetually seemed as if they all lived on another planet, keeping him at bay...and leaving him wondering, "Why? Why? Why???" (David always knew that he was not a bad person, even though Dennis, James and Dora told him that he was, making him feel that way numerous times. Ironically, everyone outside of the family welcomed his presence with open arms and told him what a lovely, kind and loving person he was. Way down deep in his soul, David had a sense, even though he had always had a hard time in grasping it, that Dennis was really and positively not David's father...regardless of the many times he was told this.)

As Elaine in her descriptive analogy, remembers David's feelings, she refers to the several occasions when he tried to connect with them, and that it was "like calling an office and the boss was out of town." He had almost no connection, even though he tried so hard to create one but was repeatedly left baffled and worn out from trying. Undoubtedly, David made a huge undertaking to engage in a family that didn't seem like his own family at all.

Quite critically, David also had no idea at all about what it was like to have a loving family feeling in being together as a family. And, when he heard that other families loved their families with great warmth and intensity and could not live without each other, he could not comprehend that, as he did not know what it meant. In fact, he had never really concentrated on his thoughts about it or mentioned outwardly that he loved his family. He surmised that he was subconsciously pushing into his heart to love them all, but it was an exhausting effort…a one way street.

And, Dora, presumably being the protector of the whole family, spent most of her time giving David excuses for why he could not see everyone and why it was not right. And, any attention that he did receive from her directly was just a "pacifier" to always keep David out of the circumference.

In David's looking hard in the face of his existence, the sheer truth and substantiality was that there was no reason in the world that that family should have made him feel disowned. There never was, and still never is anything wrong with David, apart from the fact that he, and his future self as Elaine, had always been a very loving, caring and supportive human being. And, they (Dennis and the kids) were always very cold and distant and uncaring. Even though Dora had a way of putting on a "plastic" show of care, it was easily discernable as being fake.

Nostalgia and Memories in Making

Before David and Susan met up in Colchester, David spent two nights with his former sister, Dora in her home in the same town, known as the main army barracks to Germany, Iraq and other military destinations. He was not only settling in after jet lag but refreshing in the anticipation of meeting Susan. While there, David had the distinct, emotional event of going to his mum, Mildred's grave. He brought various flowers, placing them on her special spot. It was quite a moving time at the grave site as David spoke to her about the past, the present and the future.

Next in priority after visiting his mum's place of rest was revisiting the park in Coggeshall where David loved swinging on the swings as a kid. He walked to the park, reminiscing about the past and retracing his steps. This was the place where David used to swing, laugh and sing! He found ladies swinging on the same swings and laughing with each other just like the old days. To his surprise and astonishment, these ladies were the same girls that David experienced this with at this same spot growing up! And also, there were parents of the other kids there that David knew! He asked them, "Do you know who I am?" And, the response was, "What is your last name?" David answered, "My adoptive name was Boden, but my name growing up was Mower. My dad's name was Dennis from Tey Road…"

They immediately pointed to an older woman who looked like David's mother, whom he had never seen before. They referred to the fact that she was a Mower. He walked up to her and said, "So, you are a Mower?!" She said, "Yes!" David replied, "I'm Dennis's child." She emphatically looked at him with a secretive, yet direct look and stated "You were never a Mower!" David kept a brave face, held on to his dignity and slowly walked back along the park trail to the road, while crying. He was thinking in his muddled mind all over again about how much he felt that he did not exist. He thought the ladies were probably wondering why he left so abruptly, but he wanted to cry and he did not want them to see him crying.

In wiping his eyes and in the process of cheering himself up, David ventured to Norman's Sweet Shop. It was not only still there, but it still had the same owner and the same good old sweets!

Next stop was to meet Susan!!! There she was sitting in the George Hotel lobby in Colchester. David walked up to introduce himself. He gave her a quick hug and then told her that he would be right back after he went to the restroom. Once there, he looked in the mirror and said, "I don't like her." He thought, "How do I get out of this? Do I run out the back door, quickly run out the front door, or what?" He immediately felt guilty because she had come a long way, and he had already told her that he loved her, and he could not just run away. Plus, there was the realization was that he had previously left Dora's place and was planning on going to move in with Susan at her home, two and a half hours away in Melton Mowbray.

Truth was, he did not want to disappoint her, and he thought…How bad really could it be? She was a very pretty lady, and he knew that he needed to get to know her. So, he pulled himself together and went back to her vantage point in the hotel lobby. He said, "It's very nice to see you in person." And, as they started engaging in conversation, David started to really like her...in respect to her personality, her genuine personable nature and her beauty, inside and out. After about two and a half hours of conversation, they then decided that they liked each other. They kissed and held hands. And, then Susan said, "Let's go home."

During the car ride to Melton Mowbray, there was a mutual feeling of coziness and happiness in anticipating what the future would bring. Upon arriving, David enjoyed Susan taking him on a nice tour of her three bedroom, red brick house in an upper class neighborhood, just outside of town. Susan introduced David to her son, Paul in his early twenties, who lived there part time when visiting from his flat in town. David was pleased to also meet her daughter, Carrie who was nineteen and getting ready to go to the university.

The two week time with Susan became a favorable and pleasurable routine enjoying dinners at home as well as at restaurants, along with shopping and entertainment. Susan had formerly been in a physically and mentally abusive relationship with her then ex-husband. Sergio. So, she felt calm and comforted to have David there with her as David provided a sense of contentment and security.

One time during David's stay, Sergio arrived unexpectedly. David let him in. It was evident that he wanted to meet David. David, in his cordial manner shook his hand and made it clear that Susan was now his own and not his. Sergio soon left with his "tail between his legs". David's immediate reaction was that he himself had taken care of business! He confirmed Susan's acknowledgement that Sergio was a bastard and a control freak.

On another day, David had the chance to meet Susan's mother. They used to go to her flat or meet her in town. She was a simple lady and set in her own ways. Her lifestyle had always been very simple, in going to the store, coming back home, watching television, etc. It became obvious that Susan at the end of her upbringing had dragged herself out of the gutter and in to a better life.

Leicestershire is known for its famous pork pies and Leicestershire cheese. The area was quite old and sophisticated. And, dining out was not just a delectable experience but full of history and a high caliber lifestyle. One of the wonderful things that Susan and David loved to do was to go the general and antique auctions. While there, they would partake in the auction action while developing friendships with fellow bidders. They had a "ball" buying all sorts of antiques and treasures of a lifetime, that usually turned out to be a bunch of rubbish and crap!

In the general auctions in particular, they used to get carried away and come home with boxes and boxes of miscellaneous junk that they eventually put back in the auction. On the other hand, at the antique auctions, they would buy more of real treasurable items, such as antique clocks, framed paintings, and bits of things retrieved off of ships, etc. In fact, David's presence became so popular that he was invited to appear on the British version of the Antique Road Show. He "performed" as being an active bidder.

Issues Resurface

On one afternoon when David was walking home from town, he started to feel dizzy. To back track, on the front side of everything in this book, we see popular David who was very loved by lots of people and had many friends. And we have seen and will see many lives that he lived or was about to live that could have lasted for many life times. But we are not looking at a man who knew who he was. We are looking at a lost man who did not know who he was and was searching for who he was. In addition, from the surgeries as a child, there was even more confusion as well with regard to his gender. And, the mistakes that were made in his childhood surgery, in trying to correct his medical issues, were on their way to majorly escalate into huge problems.

In explanation of David's past and upcoming issues, it could be explained in this way, as Elaine points out: "If you were to take any woman and pump her full of testosterone, within nine months, you would not recognize her and think she was a man. And, if this testosterone was not natural for her to have, she would become extremely nervous and not be the person that she was supposed to be."

This is what happened to David! As a boy, his genitals were "corrected" to make him more of a boy, and in doing so, the ensuing testosterone should then run through his body, in helping him be a more normal man and to be able to have children. But, the fact is that

David was essentially a girl living inside a boy's body! And, if they had had the technology that we have today, they could have determined that he was better off being the "girl" inside the body that he was! And, with the proper corrections, the new "she" could have lived a very normal life without all the confusion and subsequent physical and emotional agony!

It was and had become quite clear in David's/and Elaine's experience that gender is not solely based on genitals. It is mainly based on one's chemical makeup, as well as the brain. Additionally, David felt that it was also based on the important element of the soul. When David later changed to be the gender that he wanted to be, the science was finally available. And, the doctors determined that he indeed had a female mind and composition. They also surmised that he would live a far more normal life as a woman than in trying to stay as a man, in constantly battling how to figure out how to be a man with a female mind.

It became extremely evident that David's body was struggling to fight off the testosterone that was gradually building inside his human organism following his boyish surgery. The physical chemistry in his body was in a fighting turmoil! So, now, all these years later, years of being confused and feeling misplaced, the testosterone was reaching high levels in his female makeup, and it was making him become increasingly dizzy and nervous. He had for so long been dealing with a growing insurgence of nervousness and feeling easily agitated because these male levels of testosterone were not only not normal in his body but significantly invasive to it. So, now, the testosterone that was originally intended to make him more of a boy was starting to "kill" him.

David, of course, did not know this at the time, and also, he had become accustomed to living with this uncomfortable way of things. So, he just assumed that he had some kind of medical issue that needed to be addressed. Thus, he just pushed himself onward, as there was so much going on! Yet, the prevailing and outward unknown reality remained that he was a very lost person who also had a major gender issue, and he was despairingly trying to live a normal life as a man.

Leaping Over Hurdles

Even with all of David's physical discomfort, anxiety, and extreme nervousness, he pushed himself to focus on the plan of taking Susan to America and to meet his daughter, Bridgette. Upon arrival at the apartment in Roanoke, it was a warm welcome and an immediate feeling of acceptance and friendship. After several days of being back at home in Virginia and spending quality family time together, David then took Susan to Virginia Beach to meet David's friend, Carl. They partied for a few days and had lots of fun. In returning back to Roanoke, they spent more family time before Susan went back to the UK with the understanding that David would venture back to see her again as soon as possible.

David continued his ongoing real estate business while intensely working with Bridgette as she prepared for her high school graduation. After quite a lot of work and dedication mixed with challenging components of frustration and impatience on both sides of father and daughter, Bridgette got the much awaited news that she had passed and was going to graduate! In the interim and in retrospect, David did not realize how much stress she was enduring while she tenaciously at times, yet, for the most part, reluctantly faced the aim for her eventual diploma.

In the process of grappling with this, it became apparent that David was putting her through too much pressure, and Bridgette, in searching for relief and a "way out", met her boyfriend, Jeremy. And, Bridgette had no reservations about making Jeremy aware of this. In Bridgette's young and impressionable mind, he seemed to her as the "love of her life". She clung to him as he listened to her avidly and gave her the avenue of attention. But, as an emotional result, she and her dad both felt this as a tear in the fabric of their relationship.

While David was diligently organizing and pulling together details for her graduation, Bridgette would occasionally run away to be with Jeremy at his house. In only a few weeks time, David discovered that Jeremy, behind the curtains, had a past of aggression. And, he also had an excessive possessive behavior. In twinge and anguish, David held on to his tormented temporary decision to hold things tight for awhile. He was right in the middle of his engrossed designs and thoughtful ideas in planning for Bridgette's graduation, including a very special surprise for his daughter, and he definitely did not want anything to get in the way or throw things off track!

Then, one evening, Jeremy brought Bridgette and a couple of friends over to the apartment to pick up a few things of hers. The friends acted like guards, and they looked at David as though they had the intent to kill him. In harsh consideration of Bridgette's rebelling and Jeremy's devious and jealous mind, David recognized that this had the potential of being a very dangerous situation. He was immediately riddled with emotional torture, as this incident brought to the surface the obvious two major facts:

1) David had so heartily been focused on Bridgette's sense of well being and excitement over her soon to be becoming a "grad", as well

as his consuming thrill in putting together the best celebration ever for his daughter!

2) But, at the same time, he also was dealing with major concerns about Bridgette's personal life! And, he naturally was deeply concerned and wary about the boyfriend, Jeremy and his problematic dysfunctional, if · not malfunctional, history.

In the highest regard and with parental respect, David knew that he had no choice but to allow his daughter to make her own decisions. Not withstanding, in careful calculation and understanding consideration, he asked her to come back to the apartment and have a chat in regards to her imminent graduation proceedings.

In their visit, they conversed about all of the graduation events! This was also David's opportunity to tell his daughter how much he trusted her judgment and her decisions, in her becoming a responsible adult. The reaction on her part, that David felt strongly, was that she was feeling pushed into finishing school at the same time that she was feeling very much in love. And, the confusion in her mind at the time was twofold. She thought she knew what she wanted: To graduate! And, to be with this new boy of her dreams! In David's mental turbulence at this crossing point, he was fully aware, even though he did not make this an agenda with Bridgette, that her boyfriend had very manipulative ways!

In still struggling with the fact that he did not feel really well with increasing feelings of dizziness and "hyperness", David nevertheless unfailingly continued with the graduation plans. On the big day, David treated her with new clothes and full salon beauty treatments, as well as lunch at her favorite restaurant. The big event was stupendous, with hundreds of graduates on a big stage, each one happily receiving their certificates. "Seeing my daughter in line walking up to get her certificate was a proud day! As she looked at me in receiving her diploma, in her big gleaming smile, she was back with me as a close dad and daughter team."

After the graduation, David had arranged for a private limousine to take her to her special grad party at a five star Roanoke hotel, for which he had pre-invited all of her family and friends, including her mother and grandmother and David's best friend, Greg. In the limo, she was presented with two dozen red roses. (Jeremy had deviously tagged along in the limo and attended the party.)

After the hotel party, the limo took Bridgette, with Jeremy again "crashing" along, to her favorite Japanese restaurant for dinner. About twenty members of close family joined them at the restaurant. During dinner, David suddenly felt ill. He was having even more hyper feelings and dizzy spells. He started to become really worried. In the back of David's mind, he was thinking that maybe this was what it was all about: Getting his daughter through her graduation and then letting himself go to die. But David's angels must have known differently...

In leaving there, the limo proceeded to take Bridgette with Jeremy on a stroll to the Roanoke Star. To her tremendous surprise, they were met by the local press and paparazzi. It turned out that they had mistaken David's daughter for Cameron Diaz! This crazy phenomenon wound up being a fun twist for Bridgette! But, "game over", she was honest and relayed that this was not who she was! In due time after taking in the joy of the "Star", the limo brought them back to the apartment.

In her arrival, she jumped out of the limo in utter surprise to discover a brand new red Toyota Celica GT waiting for her in the driveway! In optimistic and ecstatic comprehension, Bridgette saw her dad right there next to the car. David proclaimed, "Congratulations to you, my sweet daughter, on your graduation! And, here's your new car, your personalized license plates and your free and clear title to the car." Without hesitation, Bridgette joyously ran over and leaped into her father's arms!

Major Decision

The very next morning, David noticed that something was different. In looking back on that shocking and dismal day, Elaine says, "There was no more school. There was no more anything. Bridgette was now hanging out with Jeremy most of the time." David knew that his original goal was to try to get her to go to college, but at this junction, he was feeling weak, ill, down and depressed. Notwithstanding, as the week rolled out, he realized that his job thus far had been accomplished.

David had come to a crucial point in his life, with regard to his daughter coming into her new "own" as a graduated person and as a young adult, trying to make her own decisions for her own life. She was eighteen years old. He could not force her to do anything. Plus, David was naturally feeling lonely and depressed being suddenly all alone in the apartment. All of the busy activities of addressing Bridgette's needs of daily life, education and preparations for graduation had ended. And David was going through "post graduation depression". His job next was to support her in a new way and to try to guide her in the best way possible. (There are two types of children…the ones that want to stay home after graduation and the ones who are very independent. And, Bridgette was very independent.)

In past overview, even though David was feeling lost within himself, he could hide all of that by raising his daughter and getting out there and making money to support her. In David's discernment, he had not really been a father to her. He had truly been more of a mother. He thinks that if there had been a man in his life to help him raise Bridgette, she would have had that tough man /disciplinarian to be there and assist through the whole "stuff" of life. All along, he knew that he was supposed to be a man but did not feel like one, and he knew that he was not "gay". So, it was very confusing. He had been strong in "fathering" Bridgette, but he was not firm and mighty enough! And there was a difference. These were two different things. (David completely acknowledged this fact, once he became a full woman, as in dating men, she saw who they truly were and how they operated.)

Hence, after a couple of weeks went by, David was more and more lonely, and the apartment became more and more empty. He was not feeling very well, and there was also Susan, who was lurking in the background. In recognition of these thoughts and feelings, he also took into consideration that his daughter needed some time to work things out with Jeremy. As a parent, he comprehended that one of the worst things a parent can do is to try to rip their child away from the person that he or she loves! He fully understood that both of them had to work it out for themselves. He knew that there was nothing that he could really do, as a dad, but to let it run its course. As excruciatingly difficult as this was for David, he came to the realization that this was the best decision!

In consequence, Dad asked Bridgette to come and see him at the apartment. She showed up at the designated time with not only Jeremy, but with four of his friends. It became apparent that in light of Bridgette feeling former pressure from David during the process of attaining her graduation, she had well informed Jeremy about this. Thus, Jeremy enlisted these buddies to come along as a "back up", in case there might be any emotional/physical episodes. During the visit, there was an "air" of impending aggression on Jeremy's friend's part. It became evident that the group was looking for possible trouble, and to David's relief, there ended up being none.

Yet, David did not feel at all free from the whole situation, as he could see in their eyes that they wanted to come and get him at some future date, maybe at a time when Bridgette was not around. Even though David had vehemently expressed to Bridgette that Jeremy had the capabilities of being a potential violator of her father in order to keep her under his control, sadly, Bridgette did not have the capacity or desired inclination to see the dangers that she had just placed her dad into with Jeremy. She was blindly in love. And, she was becoming increasingly brainwashed by Jeremy and totally unaware of the whole situation surrounding her. And, because David had tremendously spoiled her and treated her like a princess growing up, she had become a spoiled brat, out of control and was not taking responsibility for her own actions.

It became more and more obvious that Bridgette was allowing Jeremy to immensely run and command her entire life. David made it clear to Bridgette that he could see that he was a very dangerous person and could easily put her family in a very precarious danger zone. So, in

David's decision to diffuse the situation, he told her and Jeremy that he had chosen to go to England for a couple of weeks so that they could work out their relationship. In this major decision, David felt strongly that this was the best resolution in order to give the two of them the opportunity to "see the light". He did this for other reasons too. Because he was not only feeling down and depressed, but also in fear of being harmed, he was off to England to see Susan! He gave Bridgette a huge hug and told her to call him every day.

Before he left, David asked a few friends in the neighborhood to watch after Bridgette and keep a keen awareness in regards to any changes or problematic issues that might occur. Another reason why David felt that it was appropriate at this time to go back to England was because he was experiencing these increasing feelings of dizziness and instability, and he did not want it to be a burden on her. In David's mind at the time, he wanted to maintain his strength, both physically and innerly, by moving back to his homeland for a very much needed break in his life moving onward.

A Big Jolt

In England, David's life became a little bit restored again. He was with Susan in her home, enjoying his life and helping her support her daughter, Carrie, as she approached college. Susan and he quickly made friends with folks with whom they developed a pattern of hanging out and having a pleasant time. They used to readily eat out at sophisticated restaurants, local pubs and hotels, as well as attend local, general and antique auctions.

David was quite happy, and he regularly stayed in contact with Bridgette, who always confirmed that everything was "fine". Because of David's unusual and frightful upbringing, he had always learned to stay in "survival mode", always holding on, pushing forward and staying strong, regardless of how he felt medically. Yet, one day, while walking through the town of Oakham in the county of Rutland, he felt dizzier than he had ever felt before. He was used to feeling dizzy many times, and he had always turned to his self mechanism of dealing with it and rising above it as best he could. But, this time was very different, and he noticed that it was steadily in short time becoming a lot worse. In an effort to relieve the symptoms, he took natural calming pills from the local health foods store. He also engaged in a swimming routine at a local country club, as well as a normal regimen in running and biking and "getting drunk". This whole combination seemed to alleviate this condition.

David's two weeks were almost "up", and it was time to move back to the US. He was eagerly anticipating to see how his daughter, Bridgette was getting along and also how the relationship with Jeremy was doing. David was definitely very excited about being with Bridgette again! During his brief stay in England, he was silently and constantly worried about her and what she was going through.

In arriving at the apartment, to his surprise, Bridgette was waiting outside with stressful tears in her eyes. As David approached her, she was apologizing, saying "Sorry, Dad...Sorry, Dad!" As she walked her dad around the corner to her car, he noticed that the vehicle had been totaled. The destruction of the car was obvious. Yet, David did not care about the car at all. His immediate reaction was in thankfulness that Bridgette was okay. He was not angry. He was basically totally terrified that she could have been killed. He noticed that all the tires had been blown out. In trying to make her feel better, with the "light" of David's natural comedic self, and in showing his sneaky smile, his comment to his daughter was, "I've just got one question: How did you manage to blow out all of the tires at the same time?" She looked at her dad and said, "I don't know, Dad!"...And to this day, it is still a mystery.

Then Bridgette started crying again. Dad said, "It's okay. I'm just glad you're alive, and I don't care about the car!" That is when she pointed to David's car in the distance. They walked over to it, and the whole front of the car was wrecked. It became evident in ultimate admittances that in these incidences, she had damaged people's properties. David still looked at her and said again, "I am so grateful that you are alive!"

In eventual total damage, the cost was around $120,000, including settlement payoffs for potential lawsuits.

Propelled To Charge!

After a couple of days, in David's praying to God in thankfulness that his daughter was spared and alive, as well as being thankful to the car companies in gratitude for building safe cars, he then concentrated full force on making Bridgette realize how very dangerous this whole situation was and how lucky she was that her dad was able to pay out the difference after what the insurance covered, not to mention the ultimate settlement costs.

So, David made it clear that she could not drive anymore, after he had his car fixed. He gave her the former license plate from her car as a reminder that she was an extremely fortunate young lady. Because he was in a post dramatic trauma by the whole situation and also in knowing that it could have been so much worse, he could not help but to keep drumming this into Bridgette's mind over and over…which he later realized was way too much of an "overkill". He soon regretted that he was pushing the punishment for way too long. Yet, he felt at the time that he had no option, as he was engulfed in fear for his daughter, and he was majorly concerned about her safety. (Also, David's fear was escalated, as a classmate and friend of Bridgette's was involved in a car crash and killed about six months earlier.)

Later, it became apparent that Bridgette was at times secretly leaving at nighttime through her bedroom window to be with Jeremy. He was so worried about this that he requested that she come back to the apartment for a chat, as he was becoming more and more scared for her security. In using his investigative talent, he showed her a list of sex offenders within two miles of the apartment, so that she could see the dangers that were out there and hopefully not do these things that put her life at risk. He was very surprised that there were 26 names on that list within two miles of the apartment.

However, Jeremy still had a major hold over David's daughter. In fact, the hold was so strong that, as the days went by, David could feel and see that Jeremy was brainwashing her and controlling her on such a high level that Bridgette was actually "losing herself". It then came to a point when Jeremy and his friends were becoming more of a threat in David's life in order to maintain a grip on his daughter. It then progressed to the stage where he was besieging her mind and not letting her contact her dad at all. She was basically being "kidnapped" and under mind control by him.

It became a crucial time for David to sit down and have one of his quiet "sitdowns" with himself, and in so doing, decide what he was going to do. He knew in his gut, since Jeremy wanted to keep Bridgette to himself, that there was some possible serious violence coming David's way. People often wondered about how David would know what was going to happen before it happened, but it was an inner sense that he had had since he was born, and it had always been one hundred percent correct. This gave David an advantage over Jeremy and his "army". He was not about to allow his daughter to stay under these conditions for any longer! He knew that it was time for him and his daughter to move on and get the hell out of town! David and Bridgette's time in Salem was complete and finished.

Unbeknownst to Jeremy, David was trained as an army cadet, and for the first thirteen years of his life, he was in a family of decorated marines who taught him how to look after himself. Also, later on, he was trained in karate and surveillance, and he gained experience of surviving with "street smarts". In Elaine's commentary illustrating this, as David, she states: "Don't get me wrong, I am a very loving and caring human being and not violent in any way. But this is my daughter, and she had been kidnapped. I knew that calling the police would be no good. So, I decided to take care of business...TCB, which, by the way, is something I would not recommend to anybody."

Firstly, he donated and/or sold everything in the apartment. He then called in his good friend, Greg, a Navy West Point decorated graduate. David said to him, "Greg, are ya ready to do a rescue? My daughter has been kidnapped." Greg's reaction was immediate and quite staunch: He was vigorously excited by the idea! In prospect, they found out that Bridgette had been held up in a little white shack just outside of town. It was approximately 1400 square feet in dimension with a front and back door and two windows in the front and two windows in the back. Bridgette was located in the back bedroom on the right hand side. Jeremy lived there with his parents. They had one large dog that was luckily fairly docile. There were no gates or fences. They had a basically big garden that was fifty yards from the main road. Fortunately, after realization of what was going on with their son,

Jeremy's parents gave David and Greg permission to enter the home and retrieve David's daughter.

Two days later, at around 6 AM in the morning, David and Greg entered the house. In literally under one minute, David picked up Bridgette while she was sleeping and hurriedly carried her out and to the back seat of his car! Greg was following close behind. They quickly sped off out of town, heading towards Virginia Beach to Greg's home that was heavily protected by military presence. Gratefully, in quick pursuit, they received a tipoff cell phone call from someone who found out that Jeremy and his "colleagues" were on their way after them and thereby warning them.

To cap the climax, Jeremy failed to track down David and Greg. Conclusively, they found out in the end that Jeremy had returned back to his home after falling short of finding the rescuers. And, in outrage and anger, he had trashed his home and severely beaten both of his parents. Prison was "calling", and that's where Jeremy landed.

When David and Greg arrived in Virginia Beach, the "Safe House", Bridgette had fully awoken by then. She was still under the influence of being brainwashed by Jeremy, not coming to full comprehension of the dangers and risks of a totally controlled life with Jeremy. In exhaustion from this situation and in dealing with all of his own medical ordeals, David faced the realization that his gender problems had become increasingly worse. Plus, he had just completed a two year legal case for which he was a consultant for one of his top clients.

This was one of the biggest and messiest cases that David had ever encountered! It involved several law firms, several companies, several insurance companies, several individuals and a federal agency. He had previously received a call in Salem from the attorney with the opposition notifying David that he had just won the case! The attorney made the personal phone call because he had just beaten one of the top law firms in the country. And, the attorney was calling out of respect in recognition of David's win as a consultant without being an attorney!

A New Leaf Turning

Understandably, David was weary, and Bridgette was still going through repercussions of being out of control. After David's consultation with his daughter, he realized more emphatically that his job of helping his daughter graduate was complete and that their life in Salem was definitely over. To recap, David had fought for, won, raised and graduated his daughter successfully, minus a few family disasters and a kidnapping. Now, it was time for Bridgette to go to college. As luck would have it, David's ex-wife, Diane had gotten herself quite sorted out by this time. She had become married to a Navy commander who worked for the Pentagon. And, he had just given Bridgette an offer to come and live with them and to attend college.

David would never have agreed to this while Bridgette was growing up. But right at this juncture, the situation presented perfect timing. This was the excellent opportunity for Bridgette to have a secure life, away from the oppressive siege of Jeremy, to be able to continue her education and to be back with her mother and a stepdad, whose well founded Navy discipline would elongate sound and stable surroundings. So, Bridgette went to live with Diane and attended college, and David took off for England to Susan's house and to address long needed medical attention. His plan was to leave the country for five months and then return to continue his business.

David had closed down everything in America and put all that was left into storage, in dominion by his daughter. He was happy that she was secure in going to college and that he was finally close to getting his medical cares sorted out. His gender issues were starting to increase to levels so high that David was dressing as a woman more and more. He managed to hold off these issues as much as he could while he was with Susan in order to live a life that society considered normal. So, here he was at Susan's house living off the money that he had made before. They were quite content going out for dinner with friends, attending auctions, having drinks at the pub and being members of the country club.

And, then there came news that the real estate market was climbing higher and higher. At the time, Susan owned quite a big house, and they loved living there. (David had still not gone for his medical help and was silently suffering inside. He chose to put off this critical undertaking for that time being, not just because he was having a lot of fun, as well as concentrating on getting Susan's daughter, Carrie into college, but because he was fearful about what the results might bring... And, at this period, Susan and her friends were constantly asking David what was going on with the real estate market and what they should do!

After David analyzed it all, he told Susan and her friends that the market was going to crash and that Susan drastically needed to sell her big house and buy a small cottage in an elite area and put the left over money in a bank account safely. David also advised her friends, who owned many rental properties, to sell them all and stash their investment capitol somewhere that would be secure. Susan's friends just laughed at the idea! Susan, however, followed David's advice, though reluctantly, as she did not want to sell her big, beautiful home! But she continued to follow his direction, and she put the house on the market.

The house was sold within sixty days! And, Susan wound up buying a modest cottage in Wymondon. Happily, through David's guidance, she received a nice, big discount! Consequently, she was able to place the rest of the funds safely inside a bank account. Nevertheless, Susan quickly became very upset over these decisions because her first home was continuing to go up in value. David tried to explain to her that she could not wait until the very last second, as then there would have been a higher risk that she could lose. And, it did not help that all the experts were saying that the market would not crash! But, within an extra couple of weeks, the market crashed, bigger than it ever had! Susan, at this point had made almost a half of a million dollars! Unfortunately, her friend, who did not follow David's advice, lost about $800,000.

David was doing very well, continuing his successful real estate business, as an international real estate investor/consultant in America from the UK. It was in the year, 2003 that he decided to buy a Mercedes Benz. He received a big discount because he took a cancelled customer order for a fully loaded blue car with beige interior. David liked the car, but not the color blue! It was a Mercedes 200 convertible. David's new friend, Dominic, that he had met at the local pub, called that particular car a "powerless hair dryer". This pub was located across the street from David and Susan's new cottage.

Dominic and David became extremely close friends. In fact, when they used to watch television together, it was a close and cuddly evening. They used to visit different places together, hang out at both Susan's and Dominic's homes, go shopping together, as well as attend auctions. The fact of the matter was that David had fallen in love with Dominic, and Dominic had fallen in love with David. Neither of them was gay. As established, David had always been more like a woman and was sometimes dressing as one. So, the relationship was more of a man/woman relationship than that of a gay one.

Susan, on the other hand, was becoming more and more jealous. And, rightfully so, as she and David were an actual couple. But, what made the situation crazy was this fact: David was really a woman, in love with Dominic. Susan was with David, but Susan had a crush on Dominic. Dominic, on the other hand, did not want to appear as he was "gay" and having affections towards David, so he covered it up by flirting with Susan. David, in the meantime, was trying to be a man for Susan, so he held back his affection for Dominic so as not to appear "gay".

Dominic used to stay at the house more frequently, and he did a lot of helpful things for David. David wanted to show his love towards Dominic, and as already stated, he did do this. David was really and truly in love with Dominic, and they had so many deeply close moments together. Dominic loved cars, and he really started to like

David's Mercedes. Consummately, since David was in love with Dominic, David gifted to Dominic his nearly new Mercedes Benz.

The Beginning of the End

David had been longing to show Dominic who he really was and to explain why they had these close feelings together, while not being gay. This became the motivator for David to set out on a path to take care of all of the physical and gender problems that he had. As described earlier, David was still feeling quite ill, a lot of the time. So, the first thing on the agenda was to finally find out what was wrong with him and to go to a doctor! There was no question that David's nervousness, dizziness and feeling off balance were becoming not only a lot worse, but unbearable! And, on top of that, he was beginning to have vision problems.

Thus, after finally going to a doctor, the doc's response was his validation that he had all these problems, and he said to David that it was a good thing that he had been externalizing them all of this long time. So, therefore, there was no medication that could help him. He said that if he had internalized these conditions, he then would have needed medication. He suggested that his problems were a lot deeper and that he should visit a psychiatrist to find out the cause of these manifestations. So, David decided to do just this:

He made an appointment with the top psychiatrist in London, so that he could get the best possible guidance. David arrived at his office, and the psychiatrist asked David a series of questions. And, then the physician asked him if he had any questions. David responded with, "Yes, I want to know if I am mentally insane." The psychiatrist then said, "I want to try something with you." He proceeded to give David a shot of estrogen in his arm. Within a couple of minutes, he asked David how he felt…David had stopped shaking, his vision had improved and he could instantly think clearly. Then, David replied, "I feel fantastic! What has been wrong with me?" The doc replied, "You originally asked me if you were insane…"

He then pulled out a whole lot of files from his cabinet, put them on the desk and said, "These patients have serious mental illnesses. And, you are not one of them. You are not insane, and you do not have any kind of mental illness. Based on your entire medical history, you are simply a female, and the testosterone that developed in your body since the early surgery is causing all of these issues. And, if you continue to live with these levels of testosterone in your body, it will eventually kill you. My treatment and plan for you is to stay on estrogen for two years and then to get gender surgery to bring down and reduce the high levels of testosterone to a normal female level. This will solve your medical issue. Other than a couple of medical follow ups after surgery, you will be able to live a normal life without any further issues. I will give you a prescription of estrogen to keep you stable until your surgery."

David asked the doc if he could have a second opinion. With a big smile on his face, he said, "Walk out that door and come back in, and I will tell you it all over again." But, the doctor then, humorously, yet seriously said, "Because you have asked, I will recommend you to another psychiatrist in order to alleviate any worries." And, because this was such a big life changing decision, David did go to another psychiatrist... As David arrived at the other doctor's office, he offered David a cup of tea, which David accepted readily. And, after he examined him and looked over all of the medical history, this doctor concluded the same diagnosis!

David left the office feeling really happy, normal and calm, knowing that he was taking the right prescription for his condition! And, it was so exhilarating to know that he was not crazy and that the feelings of being a woman all of his life, and at times, dressing like one, was an actual fact of who he really was!

He walked down the street from the doctor's office, feeling both relieved and reinvigorated! The long awaited answer had been answered!!! He went to the coffee shop close by to have a good "think"! He could not believe how relaxed he felt and how much more clearly he was thinking! But, the biggest stimulation was the sudden "non feeling of shaking"!!! This was an enormous, joyous and comforting alleviation from so much previous distress and affliction.

Nevertheless, there was one big problem that David had not yet faced! He was with Susan, and he was engaged to be married to her. In fact, the church had already been picked out, and they had informed all of their friends. He remembers the interview with the vicar of the church during which he was told that the couple had to be accepted in order to be married in that church. That entailed being endorsed by the people of the village as well as the vicar himself. They found out a few days later that they had been accepted.

And, there were three thoughts going through David's mind: Firstly, he was really trying to love Susan, and she was a beautiful and perfect lady for him to marry. Yet he knew inside that he could not marry Susan because he felt like a woman. And, he tried his best to love her and carry on the life that they had together. But, David was secretly and severely dealing with the reality and truth that he really wanted to be the bride, and not the groom. And, in addition, David was still feeling lost within himself, and he thought that it could be related to the gender issues.

So, here he was, sitting in a coffee shop with all of these realities and thoughts going through his mind. He knew that he had to go and see Susan to tell her all of these things, along with telling her about the diagnosis, which he did! He told her that the doc had put him on hormone therapy for two years, which was a requirement to have corrective surgery. After he told her all of this, she was very caring and supportive. And, she offered to help him in any way that she could! Obviously, the wedding was off!

The very next morning, he took most of his male clothes and gave them to a charity shop. A few of the men's clothing items that were held back were for his transition purposes so that folks in the village would not be confused and/or shocked. Then, David went on a marvelous shopping spree for his/her new female apparel. He purchased a wig that he used until his hair got longer. He also bought new makeup.

When David returned home to Susan, she was crying. He knew, of course, what it was all about. And, he said to her, "Are you okay?" She replied that she had been speaking with her daughter, Carrie. And after Susan told Carrie all the reasons why she loved David, Carrie responded with, "Mom, all of the things you love about David were female things, not male things." And, Susan was in heavy tears, as she realized that all of this time, she had essentially been in love with a woman.

David consoled her by saying, "If I had been a real man, you would have been a perfect and amazing wife for me!" He then remarked that he thought they should both be totally honest and admit that they were each completely in love with Dominic. She looked up and smiled at David in speechless manner. He then said to her, "I look like a man right now because of all of the testosterone. I will not be having this transformational surgery for two years. Plus, it's going to take the same two years for the estrogen to kick in, and for my ultimate appearance to be like a girl."

David also then told her that he thought that she should choose to be with Dominic, as at this point, he could not proceed in pursuing his aspiring romance with Dominic, due to this upcoming transition. He told her that once he had the transition, he would then naturally like to be with Dominic. But, if it was to occur that Dominic was to fall in love with her in the meantime, then David would walk away. Susan agreed.

David asked Susan if he could still stay at the cottage until this change in life happened. She thoughtfully said "Yes". Thus, basically, everything became agreed upon and arranged. At this point in time, David was on female hormones, and dressing mostly as a woman. At the age of 42, David had "died". Now, in respect to Elaine's new life as a woman, Susan must have realized that her time with Elaine was more like living with a teenage girl because she was dressing up in very sexy clothes, and she was helping "her" to sneak out of the house! And Elaine was partying all night long for months!

There were the moments when she used to go to weekly meetings regarding gender transition before going out to party. All of the other girls would get changed at the meeting and then get unchanged back into the male apparel after the meetings. However, one day, Elaine pulled up in the Mercedes in front of the building, and she got out, wearing high heels, a mini skirt and holding a bag of chips. One of the girls shouted, "How did ya get them chips, Girl?" He/she said, "I got them from the Chip Shop on my way here!" And, at that second, she looked terrified and ran into the meeting in session and said, "Elaine got some chips dressed as a woman!"

Subsequently, the group told Elaine that she could not do that, and that she had to transition more slowly, as it was too dangerous to do otherwise. It was at this moment that the former David realized that he was already a girl and that he looked like one, and nobody paid any attention to the difference. Elaine now believes, in retrospect, that David at that time felt so natural as a girl in every respect, especially with regards to having a female brain. The change for him was automatically instant. So, soon after, she took the rest of the clothes to the charity shop and considered herself a woman from that point onwards.

This episode was way ahead of everybody else in the group, and she was told that she was different, in being just like a regular beautiful girl. They said to her, "We are not like you, Elaine. It's going to take us each a lot longer, if ever." Elaine sadly understood that there were a lot of diverse types of people transitioning. It was not a "One Size Fits All" scenario.

In example, Elaine was immediately like a normal woman. Within six months, her breasts had grown, her skin continued to be always soft, she did not have much hair on her body at all and she needed no facial surgery or other enhancements to look more like a woman. She was basically a female from day one. She just needed to have the corrective genital surgery. And, even regarding that, in results from the surgery as a young boy, the proposed new surgery would probably be quite an easy, yet long procedure, as she already had some female genital components.

A New Self, A New Speculation

Elaine went on to live her life happily as a woman. Yet, she faithfully continued to attend these meetings once a week for two years. It was great! She made a lot of friends, and they had lots of laughs and did wild and crazy things together, including partying all over town in Nottingham in the UK for the entire two years. Elaine says that these were some of the most amazing times of her life!

Yet, one must remember that she was still very much in love with Dominic. And, she was waiting until after her surgery to approach him in "light" of the prospect of him being her husband. Elaine brings this out, as she had many other choices for relationships that were beckoning, yet she only wanted to be with Dominic. (The amount of men that wished to date her was phenomenal. She even had guys who wanted to leave their wives and kids to marry her! And, there were some really hot guys too!)

One might be wondering at this point: How did he change his name from David Mower to David Daniel Boden, and then to be Elaine Elizabeth Boden? She did not want to use any name that was made up, out of a hat! So, she altered her first name to be Elaine and her last name to be Boden, as this was deeply and memorably in reference to David's former relationship with his girlfriend and fiancee, Elaine Boden.

Elaine also knew that she needed a new middle name. And, some spiritual force was telling her to use Elizabeth. (In explanation of David's former middle name of Daniel: The two of them, David and Elaine, as mentioned in the previous chapter, were about to be married and move to South Africa together with her family. But, David, in suffering from gender problems way back then and secretly dressing as a woman, and also feeling confused, knew that he could not marry Elaine. So, he let her move on to South Africa on a jet plane with her family. In the midst of the confusion, they were very much in love, and David missed her very much every day. This is the true meaning and reason why the former David Mower changed his name to David Daniel Boden. The name, Daniel became significant from the song, "Daniel".)

In bringing the moment forward to the present, David changed his name at the age of 42 from David Daniel Boden to Elaine Elizabeth Boden.

It was a very happy decision and a wonderful moment in Elaine's life. She was finally the gender that she knew she was supposed to be since she was born. Everything fit and was natural, unlike the other way around when he always was working very hard just to function. And it fit well with people too, as they had a liking to being around her and felt pleasant in her presence. Men who were straight often liked the previous David and did not understand, as they were definitely not gay. It was extremely confusing for everyone involved, but now the world seemed quite normal…All the planets were aligned properly.

Elaine was still living at Susan's house, and Dominic and Susan had started dating. Elaine used to secretly tease Dominic without Susan's knowledge. However, Susan quickly caught on! And, she would not allow Elaine to see Dominic unless she was there also. She remembers one time when Dominic was lying on the couch asleep, and she said to Susan, "Can I jump on the couch with him?" And she said, not only, "No!", but a big "NO!" Nevertheless, the three of them continued to hang out together either at Susan's place or Dominic's home or out for food and drinks. There is no doubt that these were all truly precious times together.

Elaine decided to start a new business. This was a business for women and with high regard for femininity. Just down the road from Susan's home, there was a vacant shop open at the windmill. It was particularly quaint. Elaine rented the space. It felt comfortable as it was located next to a friend's shop that she knew well. Elaine came up with the unique business name of "Love U Gifts". She had a special logo designed. It was a really lovely cute design, all in red with hearts surrounding it.

Elaine was so excited about this new venture that she flung the doors happily open for all to come and see. But, there was one hitch. Oh my, she needed merchandise! Now, what is the one thing one should never do, as a brand new female owner, feeling like a teenage girl, full of dreams, who wants to open a gift shop? That would be not to send herself with an open checkbook to an international wholesale product convention! Well, off to Birmingham she went!!! Within two days,

Elaine had purchased over $75,000 in merchandise. It was the most incredible shopping spree of a lifetime!!!

The only problem was that she bought so much stock that it totally packed the shop with hardly any room to walk! And, in looking back now, as the learning process panned out, there are three key principles that Elaine should have known before opening a new retail shop:

1) Only place a few items of the same product at a time in the shop, and place them neatly in an organized fashion, so as not to confuse customers when they walk in, facing a barrage of merchandise and thus being turned off to buy anything! And, the second rule…

2) Only buy on the wholesale end a bit of each item at a time in order to find out if and how it will sell.

3) Do not buy merchandise that you, yourself like, but buy things that customers in general would like to buy.

Even though it turned out to be a fun business to run, in reality, Elaine wound up with enough Christmas presents for the rest of her life! But, the good thing about operating the shop was that so many of the folks in the village had the chance to see David as Elaine. Fortunately, she never lost any friends, and people told her that she was more suited to be this way! These people from Elaine's past were very loving and caring and understanding, and they carry on that friendship to this day. She maintained her residence at Susan's, while running her establishment and also going back and forth to Nottingham where the parties were waiting. Elaine was now beginning to live the real meaning of what a normal life is! And, so many people can take this for granted.

Into Her Own

Elaine continued to run the shop for a little longer than a year. Since the calendar was drawing closer to the time for Elaine's corrective surgery, and the shop was not really making much money, she decided to close it down. She maintained her friends at the windmill where the shop was located, and then she started making plans with Susan and Dominic for all their futures.

The crazy fact of the matter was that Elaine was with Susan but in love with Dominic. And, Susan was with Elaine, but Susan figured out, more and more, that she could no longer be in this way because Elaine was now a truly declared woman. What made things even more crazy was that Susan really wanted to be with Dominic.

What Elaine did not realize at the time was that the wait to be with Dominic until her proper surgery was complete, turned out to be one of the major biggest mistakes of Elaine's life. And that was because in retrospect, Dominic already liked her, and she was holding back until things were perfect. There were a couple of times when Dominic invited Elaine into his bed, but Elaine declined, as she preferred to have a complete male/female relationship. It had nothing to do with Dominic being gay. He was not gay. He was just showing Elaine supreme love without judgment.

A few days later, Elaine had a conversation with Susan about her moving to another home of her own in Oakham, Rutland, just a few miles away. So, in that regard, Elaine would have her own place to go to while recovering from her operation. And, with that in mind, Dominic would then be able to move in with Susan. And, that is exactly what happened. In the process, Dominic helped Elaine move everything that she owned into her new home. He even delivered and put together her new brass bed that she had purchased. From the very startup of this move, Elaine really, really missed him.

So, off she flew to Thailand to receive her big transitional/corrective surgery. The surgery took place on October 28, 2005 at Aikchol Hospital in Chonburi, Thailand. Elaine picked the most qualified and also the most expensive surgeon in the world for this delicate procedure. And, the reason that she pursued this with special attention was due to the fact that she had had a prior operation as a child, a similar execution, but for the opposite results, which made this new surgery much more dangerous and complicated, as she still had inner female components that were not removed. And, the compelling job of this surgeon was to turn Elaine back into the true female she had always been. This was not a simple male to female inversion technique surgery. Elaine's surgery was much more complex, as the goal was to make her female parts to be the same and to function in the same way as any other woman.

The pre-consultation with the surgeon was easy and simple because she never even read any of the many forms that she signed regarding the risk, as she was too terrified. She remembers saying to the doctor "I'm either going to wake up back here or in heaven." Elaine had a pretty sound sleep the night before, and she had a prior visit from her friend, Malcolm. He was in Thailand looking after a friend from America. She had met him in the doctor's office, and he was attracted to Elaine. Here she was picking up a boyfriend the day before her surgery!!!

The next thing that Elaine remembered was being carted down to the surgery room and being asked by the doctor, "How are you?" The next thing she recalls was waking up in the surgery room and thinking "Am I alive or dead?" When she realized that she was truly alive and kicking, back to the real world, she made a quick look "down there" and consequently passed out! The very next memory in waking up again was seeing Malcolm standing over her with a big smile and holding two dozen beautiful red roses. As it turned out, he had traveled all over the place trying to find them.

During Elaine's two week's duration of recovery in the hospital, Malcolm stood by her side the whole time, along with Michelle, who traveled with Elaine from England to Thailand in order to have their surgeries at the same time. (Michelle had many difficulties after her surgery and came close to dying several times. She was in the opposite room to Elaine. It was very scary, as Elaine was hearing about her complications, but she could not do anything about it. Elaine was trying to get to Michelle, and as it turned out, Michelle was trying to do the same thing!

Fortunately, the hospital worked it out for having their two beds moved together in the same room. They held each other's hands.

Elaine was crying because she was afraid that Michelle might die. Elaine was also scared, for herself, as to whether she had made the right decision, and Michelle, equally, was comforting her. The doctor eventually in that respect intervened with Elaine and said, "You were born to be a woman, and your medical records show it." He advised her that now her mind, heart and body were all in sync with each other and that everything would be fine. And, as Elaine recollects, he was right!

The good news about Michelle was that she came out of danger, and they were both heading for a fast recovery. In Elaine's case, comparing to her first childhood surgery recovery which took many months, this recovery from an advanced surgical procedure took only two weeks.

Both Michelle and Elaine were then released and transferred back to the hotel for further recovery and monitoring by the doctors and nurses. The care given them was absolutely outstanding! For example, Elaine remembers one time when she could not "go the bathroom" because her urethra was so swollen, and she had to be rushed to the doctor to rectify the problem. Elaine was terrified, as she worried that her bladder might explode. Thankfully, it did not, and all was okay.

In bringing Elaine's friendship with Malcolm back to mind, he was indeed a wonderful and sweet gentleman who looked after Elaine religiously while they were in Thailand together. She remembers, after leaving the hospital and thus being in the hotel room that Malcolm said to her, in bringing another bunch of gorgeous red roses, "Can we sleep together tonight?" His motive was obviously sex. Elaine had to forewarn him that she was not allowed to have sex for at least three months. Nonetheless, he remained her boyfriend, and he still was loving and by her side. As Elaine thinks of this in retrospect, it was quite funny that she had picked up a boyfriend a day after her surgery!

They continued to stay together the whole rest of their time in Thailand. He took her out and showed her some of the most marvelous highlights of Thailand. They remained friends long after Elaine returned to England with Michelle and after Malcolm returned to America with his friend. Departing with Malcolm was incredibly emotional! She gave him a kiss at the hotel and said that they should have their big goodbye there rather than at the airport. It would have been too hard on the both of them otherwise.

Michelle and Elaine left for the airport. As they were going through the gate on the way to the plane, Elaine heard Malcolm shouting, "Elaine, I love you!, I love you!!!" There he was on the other side of the gate! After Malcolm and Elaine's agreement to say farewell at the hotel, Malcolm just could not stand it! He rushed to the airport as fast as he could to say his final "goodbyes"!!!

Elaine looked over at Michelle, while walking to board the plane, and said, "He's a lovely man, but I still love Dominic."

Home Again, Home Again!

The journey in flight was very uncomfortable, as Elaine and Michelle both had to sit in total discomfort, dealing with post surgery for so long. Upon arrival at London Heathrow airport, Michelle took her car home to London, and Elaine took her vehicle to Oakham in Rutland. By this time, Susan and Dominic had already organized and prepared her new home for her. It was a fantastic homecoming! She settled in nicely and launched into a happy pattern of having home cooked meals and being with friends. It was great!

Elaine, as her new self, used to walk into town, shop at the market, hang out at the country club and pay visits to friends. She was still on the voyage of visiting auctions and traveling down to Nottingham to support girls in transition. (This is called post operative support, in return for the help that Elaine was given. And, naturally she had many friends to visit, which she was looking forward to!)

At this celebratory point in time, Elaine was fully transitioned and feeling fulfilled. But, there were three outside personal matters going on at the same time. The first one, of course, was the issue of Dominic. The second one was the issue of Malcolm. And, the third one was the issue of Michelle. Each of these important issues is herewith presented, each one at a time:

Firstly, there was the issue of Malcolm, as this one was the easiest. They stayed in contact as friends for quite a long time, and in moving forward. But the romance with him was a whirlwind romance only. It was not in the cards for them to ever be together. Elaine loved Malcolm as a dear friend, and over a couple of years, he seemed to get over Elaine.

The next issue was regarding Dominic. There was already the decisive agreement that had been made between Elaine, Susan and Dominic that Susan and Dominic would be together in the same cottage that Elaine was originally in with Susan. Dominic, in a sense, had taken Elaine's place. After Elaine returned from surgery, she discovered that Susan would not allow her to see Dominic alone. And, Susan was making every hard effort to wind up marrying Dominic. However, Elaine and Susan still maintained friendship and contact by phone and occasional lunches.

Elaine was learning that Dominic was starting to suffer from bipolar disorder. Sometimes, he would be really hyper and productive, whereas other times, due to depression, he would sleep for weeks. Elaine asked Susan if she could see Dominic on several occasions, but she was not allowed. Elaine continued to live in her little house, realizing that her original plan to gain Dominic back later had failed. Did Dominic wish to see Elaine? Yes, he did. Elaine knew this because she sneaked out to see him a couple of times.

Now enters the matter of Michelle. Elaine did not see that it was coming on, but it was obvious that Michelle was falling in love with Elaine. Elaine had stayed in contact with Michelle two or three times a week, and Michelle sometimes came over to Elaine's place for the night, when Elaine would cook a meal. Or, sometimes they went out for drinks and dinner.

One night when Michelle was spending the night, she asked if the two of them could be together, in knowing that Elaine was moving to her house in London. The main problem in Elaine's mind was that she was not a lesbian and that she loved being in the house where she was living. Yet, after Michelle coaxed Elaine several times, Elaine reluctantly obliged. Elaine's reasoning for this was not just in loyalty to Michelle, since she had done so much for her, but Elaine needed to get away from Susan and Dominic, as it was harshly and deeply disturbing for Elaine to live with these conditions, right around the corner.

Then, it became apparent that some of Elaine's friends at the transitioning meetings did not really want to be around a real girl. They preferred to stay in their transitioning "party mode", which even Elaine admits was a heck of a lot of fun!

Elaine still had friends, of course, and she wanted to do right by them. One of her friends at the club had recently died because of post surgery complications. And another good friend became depressed from bullying and jumped in front of an upcoming train, thereby ending her life. And, a third friend, whom Elaine used to visit often, died of a brain tumor, three weeks after a Christmas party, at which Elaine was present to support and be with her friends. Elaine vividly recalls singing "I Love Christmas Day" to her at this event. She was a big fan of Elaine's and was singing her heart out with her!! Sadly, she died of a brain tumor just three weeks later. Everything had changed. It was time to move on. Elaine accepted Michelle's proposition. The move to London was on its way.

Utter Grief, Total Despair

All through this time, Elaine still had her dog, Buffy. He had been with her all through these times of Bridgette's growing up. He was over eighteen years old, and Elaine had flown him over from America to England to live out his days as a retired king. In those days, to fly a dog across the ocean cost $8,500. But, Elaine would have paid $100,000, if necessary.

So, here Elaine and Buffy were living at Michelle's, and for the time being, it was quite a pleasant time. Michelle and Elaine did many fun things together. Yet, the fact remained that Elaine knew that she was not a lesbian. This was weighing densely in her thoughts. Quite often, she used to go out to the country, sit down and contemplate about what she had done, in respect to moving in with Michelle. On top of this, Buffy was in the last part of his leg on life. Thus, Elaine had no other choice but to have Buffy put to sleep. It was the hardest thing that played on her mind, even today. Michelle was fully supportive in this whole very sad event. In regards to the woefulness that transpired next in the story below, Elaine remembers telling Buffy to go and see Dominic in heaven, and that he would look after him.

Just a few days before Buffy went to doggie heaven, Elaine received a call from Susan. Elaine thought it was about Dominic's birthday. Elaine had some presents in the back of her car, and she wanted Susan to give them to Dominic. Now, she said to Elaine, "Dominic's dead. He died in a car crash on his way to your house." Elaine screamed at the top of her lungs, "No, No, not Dominic! It can't be!!!!!!!" She must have said it a hundred times! She then desperately proclaimed to Susan, "You were supposed to look after him!" Susan hung up. Elaine succumbed to an onslaught of weeping and constant crying, repeating the words, "No, not Dominic, it cannot be!"

Elaine had just lost the love of her life, and it changed her forever. In spite of it all, moving in a space and time of complete devastation, shock and sorrow, Elaine finally got up from her crying spot on the front lawn and walked into the house to tell Michelle what had happened. Very sadly and to Elaine's shock upon shock, Michelle's reception was not so consoling. In subsequent days, Elaine and Michelle gradually grew apart, and Michelle became consistently controlling. Elaine could hardly leave the house without a major report of where she had been.

Two days later, Susan informed Elaine that prior to Dominic's death, they had gotten into a fight, due to one of Dominic's hyperactive moods based on his bipolar disorder. And, as a result, Dominic had jumped into his car and had driven off towards Elaine's home. In a more subsequent conversation with her afterwards, she found out the police had notified Susan with the news that Dominic had died instantly in a car crash.

This tremendous and heartbreaking event, to this day, still plays out a huge impact on Elaine's life. Even to begin to come to terms with the reality of it took Elaine five years. She found herself sitting at the accident scene, holding pieces of the car in which Dominic had died.

She also left the presents in the back of the car where she originally had placed them to surprise him on his birthday, and she left them there for over two months until she was strong and capable enough to remove them.

Soon after this tragedy, Elaine was contacted by Dominic's mother. She had read a post that Elaine had written about Dominic on his memorial website. She invited Elaine to come and see her, and they became natural friends. Dominic's mom was completely supportive of her son's relationship with Elaine over his one with Susan.

Afterwards, Elaine helped and supported Dominic's mother with all sorts of jobs and duties, including moving her furniture, doing shopping, etc. In an emotional moment, she gave Elaine one of Dominic's sweatshirts. Elaine kept it devotedly until she could not keep it any longer.

It became obvious that Dominic's mother became worried about Elaine's prevailing health in that Elaine was increasingly becoming more and more depressed. Nevertheless, Elaine pushed forward with her life and staying friends with this genuinely lovely lady who was so lucky to have Dominic as her son.

It was becoming more and more apparent that Elaine needed to escape from the grips of Michelle, due to her dominance and the loss of Dominic. It got so bad with Michelle that the police became involved. In observing Elaine in this terrible state, they immediately insisted that Elaine to be out of the house and into her own apartment through social services. She was moved to a flat about seven miles away. She kept her friends that she had already made and even maintained a distant friendship with Michelle. Every now and then, they would have coffee and/or lunch.

Michelle also realized that she was not a lesbian either. And, after a few dates with men, she met one with whom she eventually fell in love. They moved away to be together and to become a married couple.

(Elaine and Michelle remain sister type friends to this day.)

A New Page Turns and Flips

Elaine kept busy in her new flat. The social services did not exactly give these flats out in great condition. It became apparent that one had to take what they gave you and make it a home. Elaine remembers arriving with her clothes in a plastic black bag with her knickers falling out as she commenced upon walking into the flat. It was an upstairs unit. After running back down to retrieve her knickers, she felt highly embarrassed.

It took a little while, but Elaine made the apartment beautiful. She used to hang out with her friends that she had met previously and also with new friends that she was meeting while living in the flat. She was still, no doubt, suffering greatly from what had happened with Michelle, the death of her dog, Buffy and the death of Dominic. In the outcome, Elaine made the most of her pain by making this flat and herself as put together and presentable as possible.

When Elaine was out one day, she met a man named Allen. They had known each other before while drinking wine with friends. They started dating for a bit. She used to look after his grand daughter in the flat, and in a way they became like a little family. He was a perfect gentleman, and he took her out often. They had romantic nights together. Then, one day, ironically, she asked him what he did for a living, and he responded with, "I just take care of business when I need to." He made it clear that he had plans for the two of them to move in together. But, in Elaine's realization that he was a gangster, this made her want to get out of the relationship. This impact, on top of the post traumatic stress that was ongoing in her life caused the relationship to break up.

About three weeks later, Elaine met Paul, who lived about four doors down from her. Paul had a son, and they quickly became a unit together. They used to do all of the usual stuff, like having movie nights at home, going out and seeing his parents, etc. And at this point, as Elaine recollects, this reminds her of an awkward and hilarious moment:

Paul's dad was giving Elaine a tour of the house. As he showed her into the living room, he said, "What do you think about this room?" Elaine said, "Well, once you decorate it and get some new furniture, it will be nice!" She thought that he was asking for her advice as far as what to do with the room. But, as it turned out, he had just finished redecorating it! Anyway, none of it mattered since Paul was really a jerk, and she ended up leaving him. After the fact, though, she missed his cuddles.

Elaine continued to hang out with her friends, and on the way home one day she pulled into a filling station and filled up her car with petrol. As she was standing in line, she noticed this attractive man in front of her. She had this weird sense of connection with him. As he was paying for his petrol, he turned around, smiling at Elaine and then told the cashier to please pay for "this beautiful lady's petrol as well". Elaine was astonished and rejected his offer. But, he paid for it anyway. He subsequently gave her his phone number and address and said, "Please call me, and I will cook you dinner." After another big smile, he, Jack went off on his way.

Elaine felt so astounded as she sensed some sort of déjà vu experience. It was risky, but she felt that she had to call him. So, she did, and he made a date for them to have dinner at his house. About a week later, she turned up, and he let her in. His home was a complete disaster. It drastically needed major renovation. There was not even any dry wall. And, the one room that he lived in was reasonable in comparison.

During and after dinner, in his telling her how beautiful she was, he made nice sexual advances towards her. But he did these in such an unusually sensual way, and it was extremely sexually alluring. After the romantic encounter, he said to Elaine, "Look at me straight in the eyes…I want you to help me kill myself." Deeply thunderstruck, Elaine said to him that she would not help him kill himself, but that she would help him live.

In reflection, "This is a joke, right??" She then said in jest, "I'm not that bad in bed, am I?" He laughed and said, "No, my mom and dad died, I lost my job, I'm an alcoholic and I'm almost flat broke! Plus, my house is seven months behind in payments." Elaine responded with, "Jack, I cannot believe you put me in this position. I need to really think about what I'm going to do about this predicament. I certainly know that I am not going to assist you in suicide. Plus, I cannot leave you in this bad shape, knowing if you did kill yourself, I would not be able to live with myself." Elaine could tell that this man was very serious regarding his intentions. The problem on her side was that she was already exhausted with everything that she had already been through. So, she made him make her a promise that he would not do anything until she returned. He agreed.

In driving home in her car, Elaine asked God, "Why, me? Why do I always end up in these situations?" She quickly realized that this free petrol that she received was about to get quite expensive. She wrote down a plan for Jack to help him recover. She knew a lot about survival and a lot about human nature. And, she had a strong instinct that this guy could indeed wind up killing himself. And, if he did not kill himself, he would accidently get killed, because he was walking each week within an eight mile distance, drunk and on a very dangerous stretch of road.

She was able to obtain this info because of the questions she had asked him when she first met him. And the option for neighbors to save him was no good at all. They limited their help to bringing him food and furniture. None of them had any idea how serious this whole dilemma truly was.

So, she had two choices: Walk away, and see what happens. Or, help him. As she said before, she felt some weird connection. Plus, she had just slept with him. And, he was hot, hot, hot! And, also, in Elaine being a real estate investor, as well, she could see herself saving Jack and getting a good deal on a house. And, just as she thought about this, her mind responded with, "That is a very ruthless move. If you give him a new life, it would be a good deal for both of us!" One thing that Elaine did not realize was that Jack had fallen in love with her on that "one night stand". And, this was on the verge of making things a lot more complicated.

Big Plan

The big plan: In designing the plan to help Jack, Elaine first came to realize that he was a spoiled brat. But, on the other hand, so was she. Firstly, Elaine realized that she needed to make Jack stable, and then she needed to keep him busy so that he would not think about killing himself. So, in their continual dating, she included herself within the plan to be with him.

She concluded that Jack was not a depressed person and that he was not trying to kill himself because he had a medical mental disorder. He was simply a guy who got himself into some deep trouble that he was unable to get out of. And, the only plan that he could think of was to end his life. Of course, alcohol had a major play in this as well. He was also a very handsome, dynamic and sophisticated playboy. And, with his wine, good looks and laughter, he was going downhill fast!

Elaine thoroughly explained to him what her plan of action was to see if he still agreed. She told him that she would stay with him as his girlfriend. The next agenda was to put the house up for sale. Then, they would move to where he always dreamed of living, as long as it was near a town that he could walk to and not be in danger. Most people would think that that kind of place would be something like Hawaii. But, Jack had his mind set on being in St. Petersburg, England, about 80 miles away. And, Elaine agreed. In her mind, it would be an adventure with a fun guy! Plus, she would have the thrill and satisfaction of saving his life!

Yet, on the other side of the coin, Elaine came to the realization that this whole plan was completely insane up to this point. In facing reality, she explained to him that all of this would cost a "pretty penny"! Yet, she could not leave him there to die. And if she did, she could not live with herself. In addition, Elaine also was looking at the possibility of the two of them becoming a good couple.

In the midst of all of this, Jack got on his knees and proposed to Elaine. He said that he would marry her on one condition: She would have to keep her beautiful legs beautiful with no blemishes. So, she said, "Alright!" He then pulled out a ring from the past, a gorgeous Tiffany 18 karat gold ring with 2 karat diamond, which had insurance value of 25,000 UK pounds. It was the only item he had left of anything at all! And the most amazing thing was that it fit Elaine perfectly! Jack looked up to Elaine and said, "This is for you, my beautiful princess!"

Elaine was so excited about this engagement that she wore the ring to the weekly church meetings, where they used to pray, study the bible and discuss what had happened during the week. When it got to Elaine's turn, in sharing her engagement, happiness and excitement, everybody went silent, and they thought that she was lying. They threw Elaine out of the group and the church.

Then, heading back home to Jack, to discuss the continuing conversation, Elaine said that this agreed plan was going to cost between 25 and 30 thousand UK pounds. She said, in light of that, that she would make up for all of the mortgage payments so that his house would not go into foreclosure. One may be thinking…Why don't they just stay in the house, if Elaine can achieve this? But, Jack had the extreme desire to move away because of all his bad memories.

So, she agreed to have them move into a nice apartment in St. Petersburg, England. She also proposed that they put the house on the market, and that when it sold, Jack would give her back the money that she spent on this endeavor. He went along with that.

Hence, happily engaged, they packed up their bags and moved on to St. Petersburg. As Elaine projected, they found a nice apartment that had easy walking distance for Jack to get into town. It was also near a river with ducks, a perfect spot where Jack could sit and feed the ducks in continuing the recovery from his ordeal. He had stopped drinking, and he had developed into a happy and loving fiancée. He even found employment in town.

Out From Under

Everything was winding up beautifully, and Elaine's plan to save Jack appeared to be a great success. But there was one thing that Elaine did not count on and that she did not know, but she was beginning to find out...Jack was an extremely controlling man. In example, the statement that he made to her about keeping her legs blemished free: She came to discover that it was not just about that, but it was about everything in the whole picture, from the way she dressed to the way she behaved! He made it clear that she was his and that she could never leave his side.

This was a big, big problem, as Elaine was paying for everything, and she needed to work. This meant that she had to get out of town a lot, and she did. Upon her many returns, he became extremely angry with her, so much so that she had to call the police. They advised her that this was a bad, out of control situation, and the best solution would be for her to leave and go as far away as possible to get away from him.

Elaine took the advice and decided to move back into the old house until it was sold. Nonetheless, she continued to send Jack money until the time arrived when he was able to support himself and also get assistance from the government to pay for his rent, food, etc. This whole ordeal was extremely distressing for Elaine, as she had fallen in love with him and deeply cared for him, but his bad temper and ruling nature were just too much for her to bear!

Jack was happy that she was living in the old house, and Elaine stayed in contact with him by phone. As long as he believed that she was not sleeping with anyone else, he was okay with that. He promised to get counseling so that they could eventually move back together again.

But there was another big problem that was arising. The police from different counties were knocking on Elaine's door. What had happened was that the neighbors who had failed to help Jack were out to attack Elaine. And, they went on a vicious onslaught in reporting that she had murdered Jack and had buried him in the back garden. Upon the police checking this out through the St. Petersburg police department, they soon realized that Jack was alive and well and that Elaine was the one who was not well, by being mistreated. And, the neighbor next door was putting mice inside of Elaine's house to make it mice infested.

This made the reason clear why they were not helping Jack at all. One of the neighbor's plans was to buy Jack's home cheap for one of their family members. But because Elaine was in the picture, that plan was foiled. So, she wound up sitting in the mice infested home waiting for an offer on the property. And, it was not too long before she got a full offer! She called Jack and said that she sold the house and that together they would make 60,000 pounds!!!

To Elaine's surprise, he said, "Don't give me any money! You keep the money, Elaine, as if it was mine, I would use it again for alcohol and die. My life is happy now with what I do receive, and I do not need anything extra." He then asked, after she sold the house, if she would come back home? She said that she would consider it. She also said that she did not want his portion of the money. Thus, she planned to put his portion in the bank and sending him little checks over a period of time until the balance reached zero.

But, Jack did not want that. He did not want any money at all. He was pleased with the money that he was already receiving and did not want to get any more for two reasons: One, because he might start drinking again. But the main reason was that he would ultimately lose his government benefits if he got any extra income.

Elaine was distraught by all of this! It was a bad relationship, and she did not want to keep his portion of the money on the house. So, she delayed the sale of the house. In doing this, she could really think about the whole situation. She wanted to get the $30,000 back that she had already spent, but she did not want to spend his money. And, she would have had to go and pick up him up from his home in St. Petersburg and bring him to the closing. And, this was also a very stressful situation.

In any account, while Elaine was waiting to make a decision and while delaying the closing, fate stepped in and the real estate market crashed overnight. This reduced the house value by 80,000 UK pounds. This made the buyer back out of the deal. And, now Elaine was in a 20,000

UK pounds negative equity. And, for some strange reason, she was happy about all of this! She had just lost 30,000 UK pounds, but she was free from Jack's "controllingness". And, now she did not have to deal with his money and feel guilty by keeping it! She made the decision to let the house go into foreclosure. That meant that Elaine could stay there for over a year without paying any mortgage payments. And, this decision would help regain at least some of the money.

She called Jack by phone and told him what had happened. He was not angry about the money, but he was very irate that she was going to remain in the house and not return to him. And, due to this fury, she knew that she could never, ever go back to him! Elaine had done her job!...Jack was okay!

(In realization later on, when they ran Elaine's DNA in 2017, she found out the reason why she and Jack felt so close: It was because he was her distant cousin. But, she did not know it at the time. She almost married her cousin.)

Another Paul

Elaine continued to live her life in the house being emotionally attacked by a couple of neighbors. But things were not all that bad. She had a few friends too. Several months down the road, Elaine met another Paul. He knew her when she met the first Paul, because he lived next door. The new Paul also well understood that she would never date someone when she was with somebody else. But, now here she was being single and living on her own in the house. He enticed her with a tasty steak dinner at the local pub. It was very appetizing, and she did not refuse. They had a pleasantly wonderful evening, and it ended up with the two of them being together.

A few weeks later, Paul moved out of his apartment and moved into the house with Elaine. He also moved in to protect her because of the former problems that Elaine had with the neighbors. They were beginning to have a nice life together. They shared lots of fun and laughter as well as many new friends.

Paul had a mother who lived in a nursing home, and they used to go and visit her every Saturday. They would take her out and go downtown shopping and/or visiting the local pub. They would typically spend many hundreds of hours talking and laughing with Paul's mom in her nursing facility. His mom was in her eighties. She had heart problems and diabetes and subsequent loss of both of her legs. She was a really wonderful and precious lady, and she and Elaine developed a loving relationship. She treated Elaine as though she was her daughter-in-law.

Her life at this time was quite stable, despite periodic phone calls from Jack in a drunken rage. Elaine was continually missing her dog, Buffy, and in consideration of that, Elaine and Paul decided to get another dog. They both realized that a shih tzu canine would be the perfect fit, as Elaine had always thought about how much fun it would be to have one!

Normally, she would go and check out the animal shelter for a dog, because she had always been a big animal supporter, and her foundation donated money for causes for animal welfare on a yearly basis. Yet, Elaine chose to look inside a newspaper about dogs for sale. The reason she made this decision was because she knew that she could not find this type a dog in an animal shelter, or it would be very hard. And, the great thing about finding a dog in a dog newspaper is that many of these dogs were being sold because they could not be looked after any longer due to many circumstances, and in a sense, many were pre-animal shelter dogs.

In Elaine and Paul's process of sifting through the dog newspaper, they discovered that there were hundreds of dogs of this type for sale. And, Elaine felt, in a way, guilty, as she did not want to pick out the prettiest one and leave all the others behind, without knowing more about them. So, she picked out the one listing that had no photo at all.

Interestingly, all of the other dogs with pictures were selling for anywhere between 1500 and 3000 pounds. And, this one had no photo and was going for 200 pounds. The listing further said that this particular shih tzu had been returned three times because of its aggressive habit of chasing cats. And, now the owner was feeling desperate since she had been having to keep it in a small cage outside in all kinds of weather conditions.

Elaine took one look at Paul and emphatically declared, "We are gonna go rescue this little shih tzu!" He noddingly and happily agreed. They then found out that this little "cat snatcher" was living 250 miles away!

So, off they hustled to the ATM machine to capture the cash and then pursue their round trip, a five hundred mile journey to pick up this lucky dog and return home with it!

Right before they made their arrival at the dog owner's home, they called to let the lady know that they were about to get there. She said, "Oh, no! That's my friend's house! I will meet you at the service station." They arrived, and there was the dog sitting in the back seat of the car with no leash, no collar and no toys! In fact, no nothing at all! Elaine asked the woman if she had any papers on the dog, and she said that she would mail them to her. Elaine then asked if the dog, which was a boy, had a name, and she replied that it was "Quaver", named after the crisps that he loved to eat! She asked Elaine if she liked him, and Elaine said, "I love him!" The woman then proclaimed, "Good, because you can't bring him back because that would be the fourth time!" Elaine shook her head and agreed.

The lady then offered to put Quaver into Elaine's car, since, as she had stated, the dog could get frightened and possibly be aggressive. At that moment, the dog looked at the previous owner and immediately pounced into Elaine's arms and started licking her face! This dog knew exactly what owner he wanted. The woman started crying. Elaine gave her a hug and said goodbye.

So, there they were with a beautiful black dog that hated cats! The reason that Paul stayed sitting in the car was because Elaine had told him that the dog did not like cats or men and needed to get used to Paul. Well, as soon as Quaver was placed in the back seat of Elaine's car, he jumped into the front seat on to Paul's lap, licking his face, profusely! And Quaver stayed there all of the way home. Paul looked at Elaine and said, "So, this dog doesn't like men, huh?" Elaine just gave him a wicked smile.

Elaine really wanted to have a light brown dog, but this black one was okay. After a few stops on the way home to use the bathroom, they finally made it back. The first thing that the two of them did upon arriving at home was to take Quaver and have him bathed and groomed. When they went to pick him up from the groomers, they found that Quaver was a stunning mix of a light brown and white dog. They realized that Quaver only appeared black because of an accumulation of dirt on his body. It became a happy note that Quaver made a wonderful addition to the family. And, on a nice extra note, Paul's mother, Beatrice absolutely loved Quaver, and Quaver helped make major improvements to her health!

Back and Forth

Elaine, Paul and Quaver continued to live as a family. Then relationship issues started to crop up. Elaine had been through too much to at that time join hands with Paul. And because Elaine had no desire to marry at that time, they split up. A few weeks later, Elaine met Simon, and it was a whirlwind romance. She met him online. They first met in a restaurant, and he was the most handsome man she had ever seen. He took her hand and wined and dined her like she had never undergone before. She was smothered in red roses on a constant basis. He always took Elaine out to the most lavish places. He also took her to meet his family. He was the most amazing lover. The relationship seemed perfect.

One Saturday night in a lavish, upscale restaurant, he got on his knees and proposed marriage by placing an engagement ring on her finger. She looked at him lovingly and said, "Yes!" She ended up moving in with Simon. Life was very good and loving. That was until one day that Elaine discovered that Simon was not who he claimed to be! He had abandoned his wife and three children. And, he had a criminal past! Elaine figured all this out, as she put her investigative background to use and discovered who he really was.

On a trip down to see one of his cousins, Elaine finally conjectured that she just could not live with these lies anymore. She confronted him on this trip to visit his cousins that she was leaving him and that she was also leaving him there. She then ran to her car and drove off at a high speed to gather her things. She remembers after loading the last bits in the car that this girl behind her was shouting out, "I've been there, Baby! You leave that bastard!"

Paul had been constantly calling Elaine in asking her to come back home. And, Elaine finally agreed. Upon arrival back home to Paul, they really did not talk about it. They just got on with their life as always. They continued the pattern of going to visit Paul's mom, and unfortunately, she was getting worse. Plus, the house was about a month away from foreclosure. It was time to make some very serious decisions.

After a comprehensive conversation with Paul at a local pub, he expressed his real dream of moving to Wales. Elaine asked him about his current job and all of the longevity and benefits that he would be losing. He responded that after his mom died, he wanted to just scratch it all and start a new life in Wales. Elaine knew that he simply could not afford to make a giant move like this! But, the words of his mother kept haunting Elaine. She said, "As long as my Paul is with you, I know he will be okay after I'm gone." At that time, she did not have the heart to tell her that she did not truly love him in the way that she should. Yet, hauntingly and profoundly, in looking back later, Elaine doubted if she could ever find a man as good as Paul. At that point, she finally fell in love with Paul.

Hence, as a result of Elaine getting to work and making calls to a few friends and colleagues, she was able to find a bungalow in Wales that was not too far from the ocean. When Elaine broke the good news,

Paul was ecstatically happy! They both agreed that she would go down to the new home and get everything ready. And, as part of this agreement, she would return on weekends to see Paul and his mother. Upon Paul's one month notice from his job, he would then move on down to Wales and be with Elaine. And they would both travel to visit Paul's mother every weekend, as usual, in a four hundred mile round trip.

Sadly, within the final days that Paul could stay at the old house before it went into foreclosure and also within his final days at work, his mom passed on. Fortunately, Paul had the fulfillment of seeing his mother one last time before she passed. It was on a Friday night when Elaine was in Wales making preparations on the new house. Elaine feels forever sad to this day that she never had the chance to say goodbye.

Paul then came home to Wales, and together, Elaine and Paul planned his mother's funeral. Elaine had created a beautiful and comfortable home for him and Quaver, and at least he was living where he so much wanted to retire. Happily, Paul found a new job within two weeks, and Elaine, Paul and Quaver were very content again. They bought a couple of bikes and a car, and they developed a habit of taking Quaver to the beach on an often basis. Sometimes, they would ride their bikes as many as 25 miles away. They lived the free and happy beach life style, also with an abundance of seeing friends, going to pubs and restaurants and shopping. It was truly an amazing and satisfying time.

But, little did they know what the future had in store! It was obvious now that Elaine's gender issues had long vanished into the past, and that she was just a regular girl, like anyone else. But she still had long lost dreams of becoming a singer.

So, in 2011, Elaine Boden chose the stage name "Elainee". (She did not include the last name, as she still felt lost and was still searching for who she really was.) She started singing her teenage idol, Cliff Richard's songs, such as "Living Doll" "Theme for a Dream", "The Young Ones" and "Traveling Light". It was a wonderful, fulfilling experience for her, in living out her dreams. She sang at packed venues and was told that she was on her way to stardom.

Along the way, Elaine realized that her creativity stretched further than cover songs. So, she began to write her own songs and search for new songs by other songwriters. She went to work online to search for the perfect songwriter…and, Voila!!!…there she was!…Irene! Elaine had put a notice out on Linkedin through the "Songwriting Industry" grouping, stating that she was a singer in England looking for original songs to perform. Irene Leland in St. Louis, Missouri found the posting to her delight and responded right away, sending Elaine a couple of her songs. Bingo! On June 12, 2012, a musical match was made! And also the beginning of a deeply treasured friendship!

Elaine and Irene hit it off spontaneously upon the first phone call. Elaine made it clear that she was overjoyed with Leland's songs, commenting that Irene was a brilliant songwriter and that she was very interested in signing on her songs. In satisfaction and gradual development, Irene continued to send along more of her originals, which Elaine also fell in love with! A mutual agreement transpired for

Elaine and Irene to co-sign ten of Irene's folk/pop songs on a 50/50 publishing deal with Irene as writer and Elaine as performer.

Nevertheless, the other missing and most major long sought after reality for Elaine was… Who really was she?… And, why were her heart and soul still so dramatically and increasingly searching for the answers?…

Awakening in Truth

Well, in this little bungalow on 34 Regent Road in Rhyl, North Wales, the truth was about to unfold and set Elaine free forever…

Here we are now at this remarkable and transcending point in time, as shown in this true story's "Intro". Herewith, Elaine's history has been spoken. Her journey, thus far, in her formidable and unusual life is on the clear table. Now, this renaissance unfolds:

From being a lost child and in remembering looking over the motorway bridge watching cars spin off into the distance, Elaine recalls thinking so vividly…"I don't belong here." And, she knew in a deep sense that somewhere on that road in the distance was where she was meant to be. She consciously thought it was kind of strange thinking this at the time because she was actually a really happy kid. But, in looking forward since that dynamic metaphysical inner sense, she had many other spiritual happenings that occurred to her as the future moved on.

There were strange situations where people would stop her when she was David on the street and tell him that he was a special child. And, Elaine remembers one significant time, in being a kid as David, when he went to church on his own on an "off Sunday" day when the church was empty. He was kneeling at the altar in deep thought and prayer, when he imminently had a strong awareness that he was being surrounded by a comforting protection. And then he heard the glorious sound of singing!

Upon opening his eyes and looking in front of him, he saw three angels, tall and white and magnificent, standing together in a row before the altar, and it was their voices that were singing. David was immediately enveloped in a tranquilizing and revitalizing immersion. But, at the same time, he felt an overwhelmingly frightened reaction. He jumped up and quickly raced down the church aisle and ran away, only to end up coming back, not long after, to discover that everything was normal again inside the church.

And, as he grew up to become a teenager, the closeness with father, Elvis Presley was extremely strong. It was nothing at all like being a fan with regard to his music. It was something very deep inside of both father and offspring…a natural connection…so much so that David knew when his dad was in grave danger. And, in making a phone call as a young teenager to try and save his life, it was from a natural child's point of view, in knowing that this powerful link in essence existed.

Feeling frightened for Elvis and his health, about four years before he died, Elaine glowingly relives at age 13 when she, as David, made this important phone call to Elvis. David was with his friend, Wayne when the call was made inside the phone box, outside of St. Peter's School in Coggeshall. The phone boxes in those days had an A and B button that one pushed in order to get in touch with the operator after dialing "O" and then putting in the money. Listed numbers would go straight through, and unlisted numbers required permission to talk. David never had much change, so he was concerned that he would not get through…

Surprisingly, the phone rang, and a man answered. David said, "Can I speak with Elvis Presley, please?" He said "Who are you and where are you calling from?" David said, "I am David from Coggeshall, England." He said, "Wait a minute." And then Elvis came to the phone. David said, "Hello, I don't have much time on this call, but I am worried about you." Elvis said, "Don't worry about me, I'm alright." David then said, "But, I am." Knowingly, at that second, Elvis responded with "Just live your life and be happy. I will be there for you when you need me." And then the phone cut off, as the money ran out.

And, as it got closer to 1977, Elaine, in David's shoes, had a really bad feeling that Elvis would die. He knew that he could not get to him, as much as he desperately wanted to. David wanted to go to Graceland, but he did not have the money. David felt truly and devastatingly helpless. He could feel Elvis' pain and "lostness". It was an agony that no child should bear. Knowing that David and Elvis had a spiritual connection, David lay in his bed and traveled to Elvis within his mind. Elvis told him the same thing that he told David on the phone…that he is okay. But even though he knew he wasn't okay, there was nothing more that David could do. And, he hoped at this point and thought that his dad would turn his life around. But sorrowfully, he did not. Elvis passed on to God's kingdom.

And on that day, August 16, 1977, David found himself feeling so angry with him for not changing his life that he shouted out on his knees, "What the hell is going on? Why do I have this strong connection? Why do I even care?" And, at that moment, the path of David's life took a dramatically different direction away from his father, as not to feel this pain with terrifying feelings of closeness to a man that he never even knew. It was at this point, of travelling down a separate road, that Elaine now realizes that she, as David had become so very lost, as opposed to before when his dad was alive, and he was fine.

In afterthought, now he became scared…What did Elvis know that David did not know? And, what was going to happen to him in the future when he would need him? He was told that Elvis had died from an overdose of drugs. David felt that he had died of a broken heart which brought on a heart attack.

This immediately made David never want to ever take drugs. And, he also followed his idol, Cliff Richard's clean lifestyle. He did everything he could to get away from the attachment he had with Elvis Presley. It just felt weird, and he was scared of it, as he did not know the reasons.

Jumping on back/up now to May 6, 2013:

Elaine had been on such a long, exhausting search in finding out who she really was. But what she did not realize was that she was herself all along, and that the man she was running away from for so long was not the answer. And, she found this out firstly, not by DNA at all, but by giving up trying to figure out who she was and why she was so lost.

She was so overwhelmingly fatigued with constantly searching to find out who she was that on this one day, she sat down and had a meeting with herself and with God: "Oh God, I've been on a long journey trying to find myself. I don't know who I am, and I don't think I ever will. I've always wanted to be a singer, and that's what I shall be, Elainee. And, so now, I will make my fans to be as my family, and I will sing to make people happy, in taking away the pain of my "lostness" and pouring it into my songs. So, right now, I am making this decision to give up and not try to find myself any longer."

Within a second therewith, just as she was thinking about continuing her life this way, her father, Elvis Presley appeared vividly in her mind, and he said, "This is the time that I have come to bring you home….and this is who you are." He further told her to go and sing one of his songs, and then she would know. She did just that right away, going into the next room to sing! As she walked up to the microphone, she was thinking, "This is crazy!" Then she came back to her spot on the couch…And something had happened to her…Something had movingly changed in her life! She eminently had instant confidence, which before, during all of her life, especially after the death of her father, was so hard for her to gain! And, she never could. But now, she had this wonderful sense of security and self.

It was as if she had been on a fast moving train, and now suddenly it had stopped, and she was home at Graceland. All of the thousand

207

pieces of her life kind of flew together at this magical moment, and everything instantly made sense. She knew who she was, and she knew who she looked like, whereas before, she had no idea. Elaine's search was now over. She was she. And, she stood up and shouted, "Oh, my God, I'm Elvis Presley's other daughter, the real thing!" And, she was immediately so excited that she wanted to test her real self, and so she called a bunch of her friends!

She told each of them that she had something important to tell them and that they would probably think she was completely insane. She told them that she had just figured out that she was Elvis Presley's child. None of them was surprised. And they all responded, "I believe you." And when she later met up with them, they could hardly recognize her due to her new confidence! She well remembers singing a song in a bar, and when she got off stage, the manager said, "How come you are so much like Elvis?" And, she replied with, "That's because I'm Elaine Presley." She remembers walking down the sidewalk afterwards and feeling so incredibly confident in knowing herself!

And that remarkable moment of Elaine's father "bringing her home" became the moment that her road and her dad's road rejoined together! And, she knew without a single doubt that the feeling she had for Elvis as a child was the same feeling coming into fruition. But, this time, she was not scared and bewildered at all, as she knew that that feeling was because Elvis was her father. And, Elaine perpetuates in feeling and knowing that her real dad, Elvis is inside her and will be for the rest of her life and beyond. "I am home."

One of the most wonderful things that she came to recognize was that the uncomfortable feelings that she had with her other "father" were not family feelings like she thought they were. And this was a big relief... knowing that the feelings she had with Elvis were what the real family feelings were all about. And now that all these puzzle pieces finally fit together now, and she could understand why people truly loved their families in a regular, integrated way. She loved her family in just this way. She really was home!

Interestingly, Elaine's sister, Lisa Marie at this time was living in the United Kingdom, having moved from Los Angeles, California to start a new life. (Lisa was only about an hour away from Elaine.) And, Elaine was about to "move home" to Graceland to start her own new life. What a destiny in the crisscrossing of two sisters!

After Elaine's phenomenal realization and her joyous speaking to her friends, she strongly felt that the next step for herself was to call Dora and to confront her, as Elaine had always been showing love to her and James in the family and never really feeling it in return. She knew that it was not normal, but the big question was, "What was wrong?"

So, she called Dora on the phone and told her that she had come to the realization about the confusion she had always felt in growing up. She stated that she knew what her mom wanted to tell her but never got the chance to, and also that, "It was not James who was different in the family. It was me!" And, importantly, that Dennis was not her father. And, her real dad was Elvis, from the time they served in Germany. Dora reacted with, "So, you think Mom slept with Elvis Presley?" Elaine said, "Yes, I do, and I am Elaine Presley." Dora fired back with a snotty attitude and said, "Well, you're never going to find out now, are you?" Elaine came back with, "I just did."

Later on, Elaine heard through her daughter, Bridgette that Dora had told her that she had not only just lost a father in death but a brother and sister too. Dora never contacted her since. And, as far as the closeness that Elaine had tried so many times during her life with Dora and James… Now, she did not have to worry about it any longer, as they were not her true family. She recalls that she should have felt deep sadness. Yes, she did, but only for herself, in that she had to live this way for so long.

(Onward down the road, Dora's son ran his DNA against Elaine on living DNA, which made them cousins. It became evident that both Mildred and Dennis were not Elaine's parents. But, Mildred was Elaine's cousin.)

Elaine never mentioned her family for so many years, and now you cannot shut her up!

To Be Loved, To Be Hated

Now in knowing her real family, she felt ecstatically free and happy! She wanted to do something big for her real family, but there was a problem. How was she going to come home to such a famous family??? She could not just write a letter to Priscilla and say, "Guess what? I'm your other kid, and see ya on Wednesday!" And, at the time, there were several other claimants trying to claim that they were the lost child. Some were even trying to ridiculously claim that they were Lisa! Thus, how the heck was the real kid going to make it home to Graceland?

And, this is where the big journey of "coming home to Graceland" made its start. Elaine knew in reality that she did not have to claim anything because she simply and truly was the real thing. She didn't have to make up anything, create or pretend because she was simply "me".

So, Elaine's big grand plan was to show massive genuine love to her family, by singing not only Cliff Richard's songs but her father's songs, as well! She set off to record two of her father's songs, "Don't Be Cruel" and "Wooden Heart". In searching out a studio, she found one just over the Welch Snowdon Mountains, just beyond the Snowdonia in England. The studio owner sounded really good on the phone, as he had recorded for some top artists, and he was a highly rated studio engineer.

But, just like anything with Elaine, nothing goes normally. It was supposed to be 36 miles away. So, Elaine decided to take this journey on this sunny day on her 50 CC pink retro scooter. The road she was traveling in her mind became a momentous occasion. And, while she was day dreaming, she missed the proper road around the mountain to get to the studio and ended up heading over Snowdon Mountains, which were 3, 560 feet above sea level. Of course, she became very lost and very cold, due to the height of the mountain. Essentially, she was riding her scooter in the clouds.

Well, five freezing hours later, she finally arrived at her destination. It was indeed a terrifying experience. When she finally got to the right area, then she could not find the studio building. After asking quite a few people, she was led to this little, tiny white house with sheds and a chicken coup! It turned out that this guy was no longer operating in a big studio, but in his father's house! She ended up recording both of the songs in a chicken coup! And, she was bent over, as the ceiling was too low…not a good way to sing a song! She said, "Are you sure that recording in this method is going to work?" He said, "Oh, Yeah, I can fix anything. Don't worry about it."

Much later on, after releasing these two songs, she knew that they were restricted and not her best work, due to the cramped conditions in the "chicken coup studio". The whole thing was ridiculous and could only happen to Elainee! On a side note, it took her under an hour to get back home, traveling the right way.

The next element of Elaine's grand plan was to run the London Marathon and to support the charities that she cared about! "Yah, I'm going to run the London marathon on behalf of my family, Graceland and the children with cancer." After placing her entry and being accepted, she began her training, which involved running and cycling 44 miles a day, three days a week along the beautiful North Wales coastline! It became a disciplined regimen.

In the meantime, because Elaine had released records between 2011 and 2012, and was not happy with them, she realized that she needed serious studio and vocal training. So, she enlisted the help of Jeannie Deva, an amazing celebrity vocal coach, to help her with her studio and singing issues. It turned out later that there was really nothing wrong with Elaine's voice. She just had to learn how her voice worked so that she could have the confidence to sing freely with the correct breathing patterns. And, as far as the studio, she had to be conditioned as to the studio techniques. Elaine agreed with Jeannie that she would make a CD with her vocal and studio guidance once Elaine was back home in America. Thus, Elaine spent considerable time in perfecting her voice along side with preparing for the London marathon.

At the same time, Elaine was working on finding a manager and performing live shows. Wow, this was when she found out that she had a natural talent for stage! People began to notice who she was, and the onslaught of love and hate was pouring out heavily upon her. While the fans adored to hear her sing, other music artists were doing everything they could to bring her down! And, she really realized how bad it was when she went to do a gig in town, and another local artist threatened to close the place down if they had a Presley kid singing…saying that she belonged in America, back at Graceland, and not there, stealing shows that the musical locals made a living on!

It became imperative for Elaine to have a body guard, as the other artists were tracking her down with threatening violence. And, as the fans were becoming so excited with Elaine's performances, she had to have a body guard get her out after the shows. Elaine's shows packed venues and caused a stir. It was not too long later that the live video of Elaine singing and dancing "Don't Be Cruel" at the Marine Hotel, Colwyn Bay, Wales on March 29, 2014 provoked a phone call saying that she was banned due to moving her hips, and if she did it again, there would be severe consequences. Plus, Elaine found out later that all of the advertising for the event had been cancelled. Despite this setback, the small audience that she had still rocked that night!

Elaine remembers being so proud in being banned for moving her hips because her daddy was banned for the same thing back in the Fifties! And, she has special, fond memories of looking up into the sky, smiling and saying "I got banned too, Daddy!!!" But, it was not over yet! One of the things Elaine did, in learning this from her first manager in the UK, Graham Tossell, was that after her shows, she made a one to three song private VIP surprise appearance at either a charity, club, military post or special event. and on this one particular night, she chose to make her special stop at a military club with about 200 people. She sang, "Love Me Tender" with a young man in the audience on guitar.

The entire audience harmonized with Elaine's singing, and it was the most beautiful heavenly sound one could ever hear!

Unpleasant things even escalated more when Elaine was starting to be verbally attacked by Elvis fans who did not want anything but Elvis. Elaine's bodyguard stopped numerous potential assaults and death threats. One of her most memorable moments was when she visited Liverpool! She had a ball doing "meet and greets" for fans, as well as taking on photo opportunities as well as a radio station appearance with live play. She had the thrill of visiting the Cavern, which is where the Beatles made their debut. And, she was overjoyed to find her photograph on the wall of the Cavern along with other celebrities.

When this celebrity fandom event in Liverpool hit social media, the Elvis world went crazy. And, instead of the world celebrating Elaine's success, Elvis fans and unknown executives closed down everything that Elaine had achieved and made it all disappear. Here she was, just learning what her life was going to be like as the daughter of Elvis Presley! And, as you, the reader will continue to see, the hate against Elaine would increase to unfathomable proportions.

She remembers sitting down with her body guard/boyfriend, Paul and saying "Wow, the world has gone crazy with me coming home to Graceland!"

She was also hanging out with her friends, and one of them was Barbara. Barbara had been diagnosed with cancer and had been suffering for quite some time. Elaine spent a lot of time visiting her in the hospital. Elaine had already lost quite a few friends to cancer, and it was looking like Barbara might be the next. She was a wonderful lady, and the two of them had many great times together. Barbara gave Elaine a little "Betty Boop" compact which she cherishes to this day! Barbara was the most amazing, caring and loving person, and she owned a gravitating sense of humor.

And just like all of Elaine's other friends, Barbara had no problem with believing Elaine's news about her dad, Elvis. Barbara helped Elaine on so many levels, in being a mother/grandmother figure with wisdom that kept her grounded. Elaine recalls Barbara asking her, "Will you stay here or go back to America?" Elaine said, "Once everything is sorted here, I will then go on home to Graceland, where I belong." She remembers telling her that she had been lost for so long, and now she was found and just needed to go home. Barbara's health was becoming worse, so much worse that she had to be rushed to the hospital. In visiting Barbara in the hospital, Elaine remembers Barbara asking her daughter, "Am I dying?" She passed away the next day. Elaine was by her bedside the night before.

Two weeks later, in July, 2013, Paul and Elaine moved from the bungalow where they had been living to a secure apartment with security access. She continued to train for the London marathon with the opening date of the 14th of April. She also continued to rehearse singing, taking keyboard lessons and working on new songs.

As April, 2014 approached around the corner, Elaine was ready to buy her tickets to London by train…

The Big Race

So, the big day for the London marathon arrived! Elaine was overly exuberant to be participating in this spectacular event and to be running in representation of the crusade for kids with cancer and also in tribute to her father, Elvis Presley. In fact, it was like she and her dad were running, side by side, during the whole marathon. It was as if she was his body on earth! The reason why she took the first class train there and back was because she was celebrating 'coming home to Graceland"!

A lot of people knew that Elaine was running in this prestigious and challenging marathon. They were people who loved her and people who hated her. Actually, there was planned for a young mother with her cancer stricken daughter to meet her before the run at a "Meet and Greet", since she was such a fan of Elaine and her father. In fact, Elaine had sent her a care package of toys and dollies. But, she could not turn up because of the avalanche of hate and attacks on her from bad Elvis fans. It was an extremely sad situation, not only in regards to this horrible fact that this woman was being frightened with an onslaught of hate towards a cancer patient (which Elaine thought was unimaginable), but also in the hard core realization that this was what Elaine's life was going to be like, in being the kid of Elvis Presley...

Behind the scenes, before the marathon started, things were wonderful. Elaine had the opportunity to endorse other charities such as the Samaritans, and she also had her photograph taken alongside top runners. She knew that her fans and her enemies had turned up for this event. And, there she was, throughout this marathon, running home to Graceland.

The big race started. And the celebrations began. People shouted all along, "Elainee Presley and Elvis! Come on!...Come on!!!" The faces were amazing. But, very quickly she realized that she had to keep her eye out for her enemies! And, sure enough, there was one! Amongst the smiling joyous faces, she noticed a very evil look from a man on the sidelines. And, because she was running, she had the upper hand. She knew that she could take him out in a second, if she had to! And, Elaine's hard glare towards him very clearly displayed this fact. And, then he backed off. All she could think of was, "This son of a bitch was probably one of the haters that had been attacking her cancer patient." Her Presley deep look emphatically showed him. "Don't mess with me!"

She passed him, and the celebrative faces and shouts continued! But it wasn't too long later, while on a trail during the run when water was being offered to her every step of the way, that she was suspiciously offered a water container from one of the other runners. She saw that it was in a different kind of bottle, and so she declined it.

Finally, just over six hours later, Elaine came to the end of her race. It was an awesome feeling, to say the least, to flash through that fabulous finish line! Elaine said, "Dad, we did it!!!!!!!...and for such a wonderful cause!!!!" Everyone was proud of Elaine, and she was proud of herself too! After her massage and friendship talk, people said to her, "What are you going to do now, Elaine?" And she automatically and naturally said that she was going to be going home to Graceland.

A funny thing happened when Elaine was sitting in the first class lounge waiting for the train. A man approached her, and he said, "Elaine Presley?" She responded with, "Yes, Sir?" He then said, "I only have one thing to say to you…" She said back, in exhilaration, "It was so fantastic running the marathon for my dad and for kids with cancer!" He kind of choked up, and she felt that he had been about to tell her something really evil, but he just could not, as she was so happy! And, he, right then and there, shook her hand and stormed out of the lounge as fast as he could! Elaine shouted out to him in progress saying, "Sir, what was it that you wanted to say to me?" But, he was gone!

There was a couple sitting opposite Elaine that was smiling at her. And, the man said, "How are you doing, Elaine?" She was shocked that he knew her name. And, he immediately ordered the staff to come over to her. He gave them some hand signals, and the lady staff member said to Elaine, surprisingly, "Would you like to get a shower and get into your jammies for 'night night'?" This made her feel very feminine and looked after by this gentleman, who was smiling at her along with his wife. He mentioned that it was nice to meet her and that since she must be tired, it was time for her to go to bed. So, she went on and had a shower and got in her pajamas provided to her. Then she went to sleep in the first class lounge until the time when she was escorted by a staff member to the train for her journey home. In the aftermath of this episode, Elaine remembers thinking, "Who was that guy?"…

Back and Onwards

It was a happy trip back home in holding tight to the memory of running for her daddy and treasuring her medallion, while helping kids with cancer. And she was thinking that this was the best way to make her homecoming at Graceland, by just being herself! She also was contemplating, "Well, it should be fine for me to go home now and to be accepted by my family." At this time, in her naïve state, she was the happiest gal in the whole wide world!!! Little did she know what hell was going to rain on her parade!

The main "rain" was on its stormy way down the path, but in the interval, Elaine received upsetting news from Irene during a phone call on July 14th, 2014. Irene had come to the conclusion, after careful, lengthy and painstaking consideration, that Elaine's singing style was not the best fit for her music. It was an extremely difficult decision for Irene and a hard blow for Elaine. But Elaine showed her understanding and offered her flexibility in allowing the proposed "contract", which had been finalized, to dissolve. It was a very sad day for both of them.

Thankfully, this "musical breakup" proved to be a meaningful test of the strength and credibility of a loving friendship. Elaine and Irene had been developing such a bosom buddy bond through religious and constant contact by phone and emails across the ocean. And, there was nothing that was going to destroy this solid relationship! In fact, their affinity not only sustained them but brought them even closer as time marched on! In continuance, both of them stood by each other, with

Elaine always giving Irene's music high accolades and Irene undyingly saluting Elaine's support and inspiration for her ongoing music awards.

(Interestingly and compellingly, over the prior two years, there were several conversations between them about Elaine's life story becoming a book, and Elaine definitely desired to have Irene as her pegged author.)

Moving on, Elaine started planning on appearing on the "Rew and Who" Show in NYC, which she did on October 15th, and October 17th 2014. The day after the last show, Elaine rented a car and traveled to Virginia to venture back to the home where she had lived when she first came over to America, as David, with Diane in 1984. In standing outside the house, she cried her eyes out! She really treasured that simple time and all of the family love. There were so many wonderful memories. But, now that time was gone, and she was standing in the past.

She then went on to a seafood restaurant, the first restaurant that they went to as a family. After going on to a few other places in memorabilia, she stayed in a hotel in Williamsburg, Virginia. It was gratifying to experience having numerous people come up to her, warmly greeting her and asking for her autograph.

On the way back to NYC, she remembers thinking, "I need to return to England and close out everything and then go to Graceland as soon as possible." She could not just remain in America and head home to

Graceland at that point, as she still had an obligation back in England to Paul and to finalize all of her accounts and records, etc. Thus,

due to these circumstances, her journey home to Graceland had to be delayed. Hesitantly, she returned back to England.

Venturing back and forth from the UK to America did not present itself as a real big problem at this time for this visit because she was just coming in for a couple of weeks. Nevertheless, she did have some immigration obstacles as she had been out of the USA and living in England for too long. Firstly, her paperwork was out of order. So, she was arrested at Kennedy airport, as she was going through Immigration. They asked her why her papers were out of date and why had she been out of the country for such a long time. She explained that she had been ill and had also been taking care of people who were ill. She professed that she only needed to be in the states this time for a couple weeks, until going back to the UK in order to conclude her business matters. Elaine then made it clear that as soon as possible, she would be returning to the USA on a lasting basis. With that, the homeland security issued her a deportation order with her hearing scheduled a year later. In light of this experience, Elaine felt that she was lucky to be allowed to reenter the United States without being thrown in jail. (But she knew that upon her next permanent return that she would be facing much more serious immigration issues.)

Elaine landed in the UK and went home to Paul. She gave Paul a thorough explanation of why she had to return to America. She then proceeded to shut down all of her important personal business. In doing so, she not only closed her bank accounts and her two real estate companies, but she transferred her car and all of her other possessions that she owned in the UK to Paul. Pertinently, she gave Paul the offer to come with her, but he was pure English/Welsh and had no intentions of ever leaving England. Paul understood the reasons behind Elaine's decision to return to America, and that she had to continue her journey and destiny and also be back with her daughter and family. (Originally when Elaine moved back to England, it was supposed to be for a short visit of about six months, but accidently she ended up creating a little life there for herself.)

In the ensuing months, Elaine found herself in the throws of a major business dilemma. She had been and was a top real estate business consultant with a 98% success rate. One of the biggest things that she advised clients was to never get investors, unless they could afford to lose the money. Many investors liked to play the ego game and think that they were being creative. Well, going against her natural knowledge of this and since she was herewith feeling a lull as far as real estate activity in search for a change, Elaine took on some investors who claimed that they were wealthy. And this one group even signed paperwork that claimed they had at least 500,000 pounds in liquid cash.

The big bold plan was for this association of people to give Elaine 10% of what she needed, with balance due to her later. Little did she know that they borrowed the money from multiple family members. In doing this, the scheme made it look legitimate. But when it came time for them to pay the bulk of the cash, they simply did not have it! And, they tried to bully Elaine into creating the rest of the money for them. What Elaine realized was that this was an enormous scam of theirs to get rich off of her ingenuity. So, what Elaine did was: Instead of legally keeping their 10%, she paid that money back to their parents who could not afford to lose it. Afterwards, Elaine executed a hostile corporate takeover and then closed out the companies involved making them debt free.

The last part of Elaine's regimen to close down her existence in England was to have a full physical. This was a necessity that she had postponed to do for too long, out of fear. But it became even more serious to address this at this crossing as Elaine had been feeling generally unwell. She only had two months left to return to America for her hearing session, and this was something that she definitely could not miss! The consequences for not returning would have been horrendously horrible.

When she went to see her doctor in order to get the results of her tests, the doctor asked her, "What are your plans?" Elaine responded, "To return to America as soon as I can." The doctor replied, "Based on your medical test results, I'm scared for you to even leave the office." Her female doctor then stated that she might even hospitalize her. Elaine tried to convince the doctor that these unsatisfactory results just attributed to her were because she had been under horrific stress concerning all of the people who had recently died. The doctor then agreed that if she took newly prescribed medications and underwent multiple x rays and scans, that she would allow her to leave. Elaine could tell by the look on the doc's face that she didn't think Elaine could make it to the parking lot. And, Elaine was very surprised that she did not hospitalize her.

Elaine left the office and went on to pick up her new medicine. On the way to the pharmacy, she was so terrified that she thought she would have a nervous breakdown. In conclusion of this visit with the doctor and the subsequent hospital tests, it became evident that Elaine was dealing with hereditary medical issues similar to her father: High blood pressure at dangerous levels. In fact, she was close to the same situation as her father was back in 1977.

Yet, all Elaine had on her mind was to get back to her daughter, Bridgette, to get to Graceland, and also to be with Irene. At this time, she did not believe that she had much more time to live. And, she was about to make one of the stupidest decisions of her life, and she went ahead with it! Her thoughts were misguiding her to stop taking these new prescriptions and to get a second opinion in America. The whole purpose behind the madness was to get on that plane and pretend that she was not ill. And, to this day, it is indeed a miracle that Elaine survived.

Paul did take her to the airport, and she did get on that plane. This was one of the hardest emotional moments of her life: Leaving Paul and Quaver, and in her medical condition, knowing that she may never see them at all again. She had no other choice but to do this, as her daughter and family and good friend were in America. And, it was not her fault that Paul did not want to come. She thought to herself, "I have no idea how I will survive, as I have only $700 in my purse, and I am very sick and not nearly as young as I used to be, and I will have to be functioning on the streets in NYC." She estimated her survival rate at about one percent. And, that was not in consideration of everything…meaning that she was about to face Immigration.

Without Elaine's knowledge, on top of all these odds against her, there were her father's fans calling the authorities trying to convince them that a fake and criminal daughter of Elvis Presley, who is really a man, was about to enter the country!

Out of the Gate, In High Water

The plane landed in NYC, and Elaine's mind and body went into survival mode, as she was pretty sure she was going to be going straight to jail due to her immigration issues. But, in regards to this possibility, it gave her a sense of false comfort in knowing that she would then have a place to sleep and food to eat.

So, she went through immigration, and...Guess what? She was immediately detained by the immigration authorities. In the midst of the shock, but not surprise of this, she felt an overwhelming sense of total peace because she knew who she was! And, only a real child of Elvis Presley would say what she was about to say next!: The department of homeland security took her fingerprints, and she went through extensive interrogations for many hours. One of the first questions they asked her was, "Who was your father?" And, in Elaine's mind, this took her back to her dad's military days, and she sat up in her chair, proudly, and said, "My father is Elvis Presley, Sir."

After this sequence, Elaine felt that she would be definitely headed for the "dungeon". But, surprisingly, the immigration officer said that that was not the father that she had listed on her application from 1984. Elaine then stated, "I know, Sir, I only found this out in 2013." He asked her why she was gone for so long, and she responded that she had been very sick and had to look after not only herself but many other people who were ill. She said that she did not mean to be gone for so long and that she just wanted to come back home to Graceland and to her daughter!

He then proceeded to ask about her gender issues, etc. He wrote it all down and told her to go over and sit in a chair in the corner. He thus disappeared for quite awhile. At this point, she was totally terrified that he might not be let her into the country. Yet, Elaine knew importantly that she had to be, and was, totally transparent as far the facts of her life and who her real father was.

Everybody in the room looked so strict and scary to Elaine, as she knew that they had the power to send her away! The original officer finally reappeared and signaled Elaine to come to his desk. He stated that he could easily put her in a temporary jail there at the airport. Elaine responded with, "Yes, I know that, Sir, but I just want to go home." He told her to go back and sit in her seat and that he would be back in a minute. He went away again for about a half an hour and then came back to talk to the guard and other staff members. The guard walked over to Elaine and asked if she needed any water or whether she was hungry. Also, he asked if she would like to use his cell phone to call anyone? She said, "No, thank you."

The officer then called her over to his desk again. He stamped a few papers and then looked up at Elaine, saying, "You know that you have an immigration hearing coming up?" And she said, "Yes, Sir, I do." He then stood up and said, "Welcome home, Ms Presley! The exit is over there." She innately knew that somebody important must have been speaking to them, because it went from a completely tough army environment to big giant smiling faces with halos above their heads! And, their eyes followed her straight out to the exit.

Getting out of airport security was enormous relief, as Elaine then knew that she had truly made it! She thankfully was aware now that she was on her way home to her friend and family.

This next part was an extremely emotional time for Elaine. Suddenly the reality hit her: There she was just outside of security at the airport with two big pieces of luggage, passing everybody who was being hugged and greeted back by their families. She was found herself looking around for Lisa and Priscilla, which was crazy because she knew that they could not be there. And, she knew, as well, that her daughter could not be there. No doubt, she did not have the love and support that she had when she first came over in 1984. She realized at that moment that she was indeed alone with her two bags and the seven hundred dollars in her pocket. She was totally terrified.

The first thing Elaine did was to take the train into New York City. And, by this time, one of her bags had broken, and she had to buy another one. This purchase left her with $650.00. She importantly faced the fact that she had to secure these bags quickly, as they were just too heavy for her to carry around. So, she went to a public computer to look up options. She found that her best choice was to acquire a very small storage unit in Manhattan. She figured if she was going to be homeless, it might as well be on 5th Avenue. As, after all, as she dissected…the cheapest apartment would be around $5,000 to

$10,000 plus per month. And here she was living there on the streets for free.

She found a small hostel that she was able to move into right away. But, it was certainly not like the old days when one could live in a spot like this for almost nothing. This hostel was $110.00 a night in a room with eight beds. She had one of the bottom bunks at the back. For the most part, everyone staying there were students, and they had nightly entertainment. She had a blast with the students at the comedy shows. And for a short bit, everything in her life seemed normal.

Two days later, however, she had to move out. The next place she found was in the Bronx. It was a tiny poverty stricken motel in the center of gang territory. And, the persons that ran this motel were pretty dodgy! In fact, she discovered that most people who were booked there were from Russia and other countries. And, they all wanted to get out of there as soon as their weekly payment ran out. They each stayed in bunk beds and had to scramble around to find sheets. Elaine managed to stay there for three days, and then she got the hell out of there! She did feel fortunate though, as there was one Russian gentleman who had to return to Russia in facing persecution.

There she was again on the street in Manhattan with only 50 dollars to her name. As night started to fall, she became immersed in panic, standing in the darkness with sobbing eyes. She did not want to do it, but she had to... She asked a stranger where the homeless shelter was and how to get there. In having no experience with this, she had no idea that there was one shelter for women and one for men. The directions she was given landed her at the men's shelter.

She stood at the front desk in tears telling them that she was homeless and had nowhere to go. This normally would have been a very bad thing to do because the people there were experienced homeless people. The front desk clerk looked at a fellow employee and said, "This girl has turned up here. Go and get the manager!" The manager, who was female, came down the stairs and took Elaine up the stairs with her. She said that it was late, that they were closed and there was not much that she could do. She asked Elaine what her name was, and she told her, "Elaine Presley." She said, "Wait here!"

When she came back, she sat down and gave Elaine some travel cards and money and told her that one of their security guards was going to escort her to a church where she could stay for the night. They had to walk about two miles, and on the way, the officer said to her, "Now you can start thinking about yourself, your life and helping other people." She stopped him in his tracks and said that she had always helped other people. And, he said that that was a good thing.

A Rainbow Waiting

The church where she stayed provided her with a chair in which she could sleep, and it was looked after by two security guards. The next morning, she was sent to a woman's shelter in Manhattan. And, upon arriving, she was told that she could stay there as long as she needed. Elaine was soon to discover that she loved it there, and she fit right in. She lived in a dorm with about forty other girls. They spent a lot of time talking. They even went to church on a regular basis. They also enjoyed going out for coffee time together.

There was one black woman there who was 78 years old, and she had been living there for twenty years. Keep in mind, as Elaine contemplated, that this was a homeless dwelling, and this woman had been homeless for that amount of time. Elaine became immediately disgusted that not one business person in New York had taken it upon themselves to put this deprived lady in her own habitat. This proved to be a particular time in which Elaine wished she still had lots of money, as there was no question that she would have found this woman a home.

The staff treated Elaine in a special manner, and they often gave her gifts. It was actually a very structured place, but full of love! There was Elaine living in the heart of Manhattan with a bunch of friends. But there was the harsh reality that the place was also incredibly dangerous, enclosing ex prisoners, drug addicts and persons with extreme mental issues. Contracting a disease would be very easy since there were so many sick people living there, and Elaine could feel the impending dangers lurking every single day.

Elaine had actually been only staying there about two weeks when a lady approached her with a nice big grin, and asked, "How would you like the opportunity to live in a luxury house with full sponsorship for eighteen months to get your life in order?" She went on to say that they would give her full assistance and funding until she could get her life together and find employment, for which they would help her. They also stated that there would be conditions and rules. But, for the first six months, they would require her to rest.

In awe, Elaine went to see the house, and it was totally amazing, not to mention completely secure. The total sponsorship package that they offered her would have equaled to about two million dollars. She agreed, but she expressed that ultimately, she wanted to get home to Graceland. In accordance, they made it clear that she first had to get her life straight there. At this phase, she had not spent one night on the streets. But, there was a technicality....

When she first landed in NYC, she was supposed to go and visit her long distance friend in St. Louis, Missouri, and it was Irene Leland. But she was too embarrassed to call her and tell her that she was almost out of money. She never, ever had any inclination to call anybody, especially a best friend, and put herself on their doorstep and in an awkward position.

But, the good news was that after being in NYC for two weeks, Elaine had, by some strange miracle, come to a sense of feeling so secure in that she had a very good place to go. But, through subsequent phone conversations between Elaine and Irene, Irene made it vehemently clear that she insisted that Elaine come to stay with her in St. Louis, despite Elaine's saying over and over that she did not want to be a burden on her good friend.

Upon analyzing these two very enticing offerings, Elaine made the craziest decision of her life, in regards to giving up all of the safety and financial security of staying in Manhattan with her wonderful offer! She chose to leave that behind and come to St. Louis for two reasons: One, Elaine did not like to break promises. Two, her spot in St. Louis was closer to Memphis, Tennessee. So, she was given the money by the homeless shelter to take the coach to St. Louis.

Off she went on her two day jaunt to good ole St. Louis! And she could not help thinking that her original hopeful journey home to Memphis, Tennessee, by coming to St. Louis, was about to place her just 250 miles away from her home.! So, she took the long and tedious bus ride to St. Louis, calling Irene to let her know that she was in progress and on her way!

In arriving to her new 'Heart of America" destination on October 7th, 2015, Elaine was thinking, "Oh, my, I've just put my whole life on the line!" She called Irene on what little battery power that she had left on her free phone from the city of New York, and said, "Hi! I'm here!"

Irene was so very consoled to know that Elaine had safely landed and also so very exuberant in realizing that she was about to finally meet, face to face, her dear friend with whom she had become so engaged!

Assuredly, meeting Irene was a monumental occasion and development for Elaine, but it also brought forward for her a distinct combination of both joy and fear. No question, Elaine was overjoyed to see her, but on the other hand, she was placing all of her faith in the hands of Irene.

In clarification, Elaine had always had control of her life before this big move, and now she had relinquished that control to somebody else, something that she had never done before. Nevertheless, there she was embarking on a major new advancement. Looking back in retrospect, the fact that Elaine gave up her control for the first time in her life, it was a good thing. This is where she learned to let go…and sometimes trust other people, by not always being in survival mode.

A New Threshold in Life

In the car ride from the bus stop in downtown St. Louis back to Irene's home in Brentwood, it was as if two gleeful little girls/best friends were on their way to see their very first movie! And, oh, what a 'movie" lay ahead of them...

It all started with pulling up the driveway to Irene's two story brick colonial house. It appeared as a cozy little house from the front view, but as the car made its way up the drive, in Elaine's mindful view, the house seemed to grow into another house in the back! Truth is, the previous owners, in the early seventies, had an addition built on the back end of the structure, including a brick patio. (The original house dated back to 1964.)

Irene had spent almost 40 years of her life in this home, moving in with her husband, Joe in 1977 when their son, Joey was seven years old and having another son, Austin a year later. Irene and Joe were to go through an amicable divorce in 1988 and remained close friends. Tragically, their son, Joey's life came to an end at age 21. Irene later had a marriage with Chris from 1992 to 1995. There were many good times and many hard times that were lived under that roof!.. Lots of productivity, lots of parties, lots of emotions in sadness and gladness and lots of amazing developments.

Elaine's first reaction, as Irene took her on a brief initial tour inside the home, was "Oh, it feels so very English!" This pleased Irene, as it was nice to know that the interior accents and "feel" of the house responded automatically well with Elaine's familiarity. Irene's heritage was definitely English! And, Elaine had a natural concept and knowledge of that! All in all, the home retained and exuded an interesting mixture of distinctive and impressive antiques, including English, French, and Victorian combined with bits of Colonial and Ranch elements.

(Quite movingly, Irene's maternal grandfather, Robert Leathan Lund's mother, Sarah Stephenson was the niece of the "Father of the Railroad", George Stephenson, the inventor of the steam engine and the builder of the first railroad between Manchester and Liverpool, England in 1835.)

Also, Elaine immediately, mysteriously and pleasantly felt at home and in the perfect comfort zone when she walked into Irene's family room, which was part of the addition to the back of the house. It was strikingly similar to the "Jungle Room" of Graceland, from the cedar wood walls to the wood ceiling beams to the same type of carpeting…down to even a duplicate of a lamp shade!

Irene had been cheerily preparing for Elaine's visit, and it fulfilled her that the recently renovated two rooms upstairs across from her bedroom would now be occupied. Elaine found her comfortable, cozy spot in the guest room, and then soon after, she made her office/private work space in the newly created "fun room", as Irene called it. This was a happy room filled with all kinds of collections, from foreign dolls to penguins to angels to teddy bears.

So, Elaine settled in and readily got the hang of the swing of things! Here was a new threshold for Elaine and Irene! And as things panned out, the two of them jived quite famously, further cultivating their already established components of a lot of characteristics, from naturally seeing "eye to eye" to instantly "clicking" in conjoined depth and humor! Heartily and vivaciously, the two gals shared an instinctive understanding of deep meaning in life, and on the lighter side, they also enjoyed an automatic and spontaneous sense of fun-loving craziness! Importantly, these common denominators played out to serve well in their getting along with each other and in dealing with the factors of life.

All About the Box

It became quite apparent that Irene's lifestyle was very down to earth, "homey" and free spirited! Even though she was grateful for her highly structured, fine and well protected upbringing in the affluent environment of St. Louis, Irene was the "rebel" in her family, and she had made the choice many years before to "jump out of the box" and to live in the real world! In doing so, she made some security sacrifices, but she loved being free to be herself!! Nevertheless, the elements of her family and their original influence were still looming in the near background. And, Elaine sensed this eminence and watchful eye around her from the very beginning, as she was considered an "outsider" and a total stranger!

Even though Irene went out of her way to comfort and reassure her, along with trying to "soften the blow" with her family's reactions, Elaine kept feeling, over and over, the demands upon her to be totally transparent…And, that was right up Elaine's alley! This was one of Elaine's natural traits, to be completely open about everything. And, she was about to prove it, just by being who she was: Herself. An honest, sincere and true person. (And, oh, what wondrous ramifications were on the way!)

Yet, immediately in this new living space, considering and regardless of these monitoring factors, she felt like her whole life was being put inside a box, which later on wound up being her security blanket. (Elaine discovered that when one lives in the high society framework, one's whole outside world disappears, and one lives inside another world. And, in fact, she also discovered that she very much got a kick out of living in this new entity, "living in a box"! She even truly liked it and preferred it, because it offered safety and stringent rules within a hidden world.)

Here Elaine was with her new life in sharing the aspects of the Presley and Leland families. Elaine found herself trying to design her new plan in this new milieu. One of the first things she concluded was that, unlike regular families where there was tremendous support whether you succeeded or failed, she surmised that this was definitely not the way in high caliber families: You had to stand on your own two feet, get out there and make it happen! And, no matter what, there was little, if any sympathy. Your life was on your head!

Well, here was the paradox of it all: Irene was her own rebel from her own world. Even though she was appreciative for her secure and privileged upbringing with proud heritage on both sides of her lineage, Irene always knew down deep that this tight, strict, and high living manner was not a fit for her! In large part, she felt constricted and limited by the imposed restrictions and certain guidelines that were expected upon her. But it also had to do with Irene's rightful perception of the manner of the social elements in which she grew up:

There was always a heavy weight of importance placed on the outward appearance of society families in keeping with everything looking just right and flawless. The proper image! The perfect façade! This pretentious way of life did not ever sit well with Irene, and it was definitely not in her innate "grain"! As declared, for so long, she yearned to jump out of the box and to be totally herself, a free spirit, living in the real world…which she did! And, in doing so, she found herself as she really was, becoming not only more and more on her own, but more in her own!

Meanwhile, in contrast, and as stated earlier, Elaine was now growing aware of and discerning this whole new concept of feeling "in the box" and realizing that this sense of being was so much what had been missing in her life and what she had been craving for, for such a long time: To feel wanted, secure, safe. To know that there was a place for her. To have an identity.

Ironically, the two women had the same goal of becoming truly "themselves", but they each discovered a different take on it! Different concepts of the meaning of the "box". And in the dissecting process of Elaine's discernment, she was fascinated and intrigued with Irene's starkly opposite take on it all! Thus, she wanted to know more about the framework and repercussions of Irene's history. (Elaine and Irene had a natural way of sharing their stories with each other, and happily, they both also had open ears, great interest and natural understanding.)

In this respect and in following Elaine's curiosity, one day came to mind. The two of them were occupying the library of Irene's home, a nicely nestled little room, kind of like a parlor. It was a place not as regularly inhabited as the family room, where they spent much time, or as even the living room or study. There they were in front of the fireplace. Irene was sitting in an old wooden rocking chair playing the role of a storyteller, and Elaine was erect in a stalwart yet cushiony English chair, avidly listening!

Elaine particularly noticed and realized that, in appropriate style, considering the situation, that a most distinguishing and rare piece of antique cabinetry graced the room. (Irene had told her that it was historically named the "Cabinet of Curiosities". A gorgeous mahogany massive artifice from the sixteenth century, containing multiple diverse marble inlaid drawers and doors surrounding gold angel handles as the centerpiece, this treasure that had been passed on down to Irene's family, originally inhabiting the palace of Prince Borghese in Rome.) Elaine was thinking…What an interesting backdrop for her curiosity to hear Irene's tales of the past! Feeling energized by Elaine's keen interest, Irene rocked along and unveiled memories and analysis.

There were many stories, and with each atypical one, there was a sharing and receptive connection between Elaine and Irene. Each story provided clues to Irene's meaning of wanting to do things her own way being "out of the box", in showing a powerful glimpse into the overall view of Irene's upbringing and former life. Elaine found it all terribly enthralling! And, she kept encouraging Irene to share more and more…

Here are a few of the highlights:

- Going against protocol, Irene became chums with the service people who also helped raise her. They were the cook, Clara, the maid, Lillian, the laundress, Abby and the yardman, Melvin. As far as Irene was concerned, they were right in the same "best friend" niche as her closest school buddies! She shared much of her thoughts and feelings with them, and she stood by them when she felt that they were struggling or sensitive to unfair treatment. Irene's upbeat nature gave them a lilt every day and made their jobs more carefree!

- When Irene spent three summers in a camp in North Carolina, her fellow campers simply could not believe it when they found out about her refined background. This was the biggest complement for Irene, as she was gratified that they saw her as the down-to-earth kid that she was!

- As a blooming young adult, she refused to join an elite volunteer organization in which her family had been involved on a high level for years. To the contrary, she became a part of the employment world. This involved many capacities, from retail sales to freelance modeling and commercial work to later publishing and managing her son's maze making business.

- She did not want to marry a St. Louis "Mr. Society" individual, of which she had opportunities to do. She fell in love with a very special man from Kankakee, Illinois, whom she met in NYC.

- While raising her two sons, Irene was glad to work part time as a proof reader at the family publishing company. In her natural stride, she easily became close pals with all of the employees. These friendships ideally should have been considered healthy and a good thing. Instead, it sent up "red flags" in the family, as Irene was part of the family company board, and this friendly connection was strongly viewed as stepping outside of the line of duty. But, in Irene's way of thinking and feeling, it was an important, much needed personal touch, in keeping inside the line!

- Typically, when Irene was happy to be a guest at any number of prominent social parties, it was not uncommon for her to engage in effervescent, open conversations with the helpful staff, be it the drink and food servers to even the cooks in the kitchen! The established, astringent, invisible boundaries between the "upper" and "ordinary" people in the environs meant nothing to her. In her mind and way, she wasn't breaking any barriers, as there were no barriers.

Quite basically, Irene fondly and gratefully looked back on her formative years in St. Louis, living in a grand mansion with a tennis court, spending summers in the other family home in Michigan, attending a fine private school and college, receiving a well rounded liberal arts education, and experiencing the ultimate event of making her social debut into local society.

Thankfully, Irene always had the care and firm protection within a loving family. She was especially devoted to her dad and had a natural bond with him. They had much in common, in characteristics of warm, open and fun personalities that never missed a beat in creative, synchronized humor! They also shared talents of music making, songwriting, performing and tennis playing prowess.

Irene's relationship with her mom was quite different. Her mother was a dominating and very controlling figure. She adored Irene, but it was conditional love. Irene was constantly under her mom's microscope, being measured and unpleasantly being put in the topsy-turvy spot of hoping for loving adulated approval and dreading condescending disapproval.

Throughout all of Irene's childhood and growth, there was always a powerful inner consciousness that told her and drove her to be who she really was. And it led her to take on a bold new path. Sacrifices were in the fold, and finances became tight. But in the big scheme of things, Irene would become free and ultimately out from being under any kind of rules or control! And, she became a living testimonial to the true gut meaning of real happiness, and it had absolutely nothing to do with money...or name...or power! As Irene said, "It is all about being content within your own skin, knowing truly who you are, being in tune and harmony with your soul and being thankful for every second of this miraculous life!"

The fact was that Irene's "old world" was naturally still around in the background, regarding her original family and the old way of things. And, even though Irene spent most of her later life living in the "real" territory in which she felt comfortable, a small part of her from her past remained attached. And when happenings, such as holiday family "get togethers", social events, and memorial receptions called for her to temporarily rejoin, so to speak, she could be a natural part of it all.

Elaine just plain found every bit of Irene's environmental life, from old times to new times, to be extremely interesting. Quite broadly, she was fascinated with the similarities that she perceived between the society world and the celebrity world! She found it very stimulating and helpful in her preparation for what to expect in better understanding the upcoming elevated culture that was about to envelop her!

As Elaine was envisioning moving forward in her life, within this newly different and sometimes exacting environment, she found herself looking out of the front bay window of Irene's home and musing, "Can I live up to the lifestyle defined by the big houses down the street?" And the answer that came from inside herself was, "Yes, and I'm gettin' there!"

Interestingly, Elaine and Irene spoke often about the dichotomy of their life declarations: Irene, as formulated, feeling so much more in her own, living her life on as "out of the box"! Whereas, Elaine, finding what she was searching for, to feel secure in her identity and to be "in the box"! Their goals were definitely the same, to be truly themselves!! And, both of their solutions sprouted from the "box"! But, quite differently, Irene, in seeking her goal, longed to be "outside", and Elaine, in her pursuit, craved to be "inside"!

And, uncannily, in perspective of it all, Elaine came to the analytical, yet funny realization that Irene's "out of the box" world had become Elaine's "in the box" world.

Setting the Pace

Aside from all of these illuminations and themes, the important development playing out was that Elaine and Irene kept authenticating their loyal and shored up friendship. What started out as a nice and friendly visit grew into an ongoing and well founded, caring relationship. And, along with it all, they formed a mutual support system, utilizing their individual assets in helping each other. In regards to Irene's lack of technical and computer knowledge, Elaine was always there to guide her, figure out the issue and mostly fix the problem, that Irene in no way could have done without her! And, equally supporting, in Elaine's need for literary structure and grammar assistance, Irene was there to serve her, which made all of the difference!

They also had a bolstering affinity for their music. It was definitely a mutual support system on both counts:

Elaine continued to highly regard Irene as a brilliant songwriter, and she was constantly putting her in touch with good contacts and sources to give her songs exposure. She was very proud of Irene's achievements and numerous ongoing awards. (Irene went on to accumulate over a hundred Best Song awards with superb reviews and the very highest recognitions from an international music organization/competition, The Akademia. She owes all her gratefulness to Elaine for informing her about this reputable association.)

Irene looked up to Elaine's musical dedication and determination, and she saw much promise in her unique voice and singing technique. She always got a kick out of the times when Elaine would suddenly break out into a spontaneous execution in re-enacting one of her dad's songs or creating a creative act! Irene was always there for her if she asked for feedback or tips regarding her vocal expression or guitar presentation.

But, on a much bigger level, Irene became more and more thankful for the fact that Elaine was unwavering. She always went out of her way, on the drop of a hat, to aid Irene with whatever assistance she was looking for. Nothing was too much trouble for Elaine. She would drop anything to help her! Also, without Irene ever asking, Elaine took on a huge brunt of the chores of the house, inside and out, not to mention, running errands and shopping for household needs. Elaine was a Godsend for Irene. And, without end, Elaine expressed her thankfulness for Irene's hospitality.

Even though Elaine had to continually face the challenges of being the daughter of the King, she forged through it all, and Irene never stopped standing by her and being a boosting sound board! And, from the "get go", there was not a day that Elaine did not put out her 1000 percent energy into organizing and establishing a working plan for herself, in not only utilizing her past professional experiences but reaching out in research for new avenues to navigate. She found employment as an investigator for federal and private agencies and well demonstrated her persevering and tenacious abilities in this realm.

Plus, she diligently and devotedly poured out her avid efforts in creating her own company,

L&L Presley LLC (a family publishing company) along side of her charity causes through her Elaine Presley Foundation.

Again and again, in fun sprees, one after the other, Irene soaked up the joy of introducing Elaine to her many friends, as well as family members. It could not have been more thrilling and satisfying to encounter the pleasing reactions from each of these dear persons in Irene's life. Over and over, they were all totally enchanted with Elaine! From her outgoing effervescence to her genuine "hands down" sincere essence to her alluring charm and endearing English accent to her witty, wacky British humor, Elaine shone!!! No question, she won over each and everyone. And, what was especially heartwarming was the binding fact that upon every subsequent "get together", it was as though Elaine had been around forever...a part of this family of friends!

In settling in to her new St. Louis environment and way of life, one of the major things that Elaine had to address was her health. She had obviously been procrastinating on this substantial issue for a long time. But, just like her father who had spiritually been there for her ever since she was born, he was here for her again at this time too. He showed himself in many ways, especially at this moment when Elaine needed help and assistance:

Elaine was on the computer, and a video from Larry Geller, her dad's hairdresser and spiritual advisor, popped up! He was speaking about how Elvis took too long to get help as far as the health condition that Elaine and her dad both shared together. She immediately woke up from viewing this, knowing that it was part of the roadmap that her father had left her to follow. She then did two things: She booked an appointment with a doctor, and then she contacted Larry Geller to thank him for the informative video! In this process, they talked about not only this as a "meant to be" video but, she thanked him for saving

her life! And, he was most gracious! Elaine knew that she would always consider Larry as a good friend and someone whom she could trust.

To convey a couple of other instances of how Elaine's dad came forward with his supportive "watching over" signals: There was an old radio, circa 1960, that Elaine discovered in Irene's basement. Even though Irene thought that it should be discarded, Elaine felt an urge to hold onto it. In pulling it out of the "rubble", Elaine accidently dropped it on the hard cement basement floor. Irene proclaimed, "Don't worry about it! It's now history! Just throw it away!" Elaine, despite this, felt a compelling feeling of closeness and attachment to it, and she brought the supposed "dead" radio back upstairs and placed it in the upstairs study. As soon as she plugged it in and turned it on, not knowing what station it had been left on, out of the blue, right then and there, as poignant as ever, Elvis' "Are You Lonesome Tonight" played promptly!!

Elaine stressed her thoughts to Irene that one of the great benefits of being in either a high society or a celebrity family, is that you get the best of everything. All you have to do is make it work! (Life can be hard, and life can be easy. But it is certainly always protected within secrecy.)

Now that Elaine was taking care of her health issues, she realized again how lucky she was to be alive! And, she vowed to herself to always look after herself medically. Now that this issue had been addressed, Elaine had other major things to worry about: Money! Homeland security! It turned out that the costs for homeland security and immigration needs were going to be tremendous and would involve approximately about a three year legal battle. So, Elaine found one of the top lawyers, which was a good thing to get used to, because Elaine's life had become ruled by lawyers, confidants and managers, since she was the daughter of Elvis Presley.

When Elaine first "came home", she did everything she could to entertain the public because she loved making the fans happy. But she soon understood that the unauthorized and unorganized public appearances were to stop without clearance. So, there she sat, living in the "behind the scenes" life, feeling beaten down by all of the punishment. She finally got her act together and did things correctly through her team. And, this is why one only saw Elaine out there doing stuff that was handled correctly and by protocol.

All of the lawyers who represented Elaine were, and still are superior attorneys in their respective fields, and her personal business lawyer previously worked on cases related to her father. As well as her legal team, Elaine had/has the best medical team as well. And, the final part of this story for Elaine was that she was ever so proud to be home at Graceland! And, she proudly ran and runs her company and foundation from Graceland. (Both her company and foundation are debt free. And, by her company being newly formed, Elaine struggled a little bit in achieving to move it forward. Nevertheless, she has maintained a 5 star reputation in Memphis, Tennessee.)

Originally, before Elaine "came home", her desire was to form Boden House for the homeless. Then later when she came home, it would become "Presley House". But she discovered that her sister, Lisa Marie had already formed "Presley Place". So, Elaine thus established "Elaine Presley Wish Foundation". This, by the way, is just one of many examples of how Elaine and her family have always been on the same wave length.

Homeward to Graceland

Elaine was in wonder and magical expectation of taking the long anticipated trip to her "homeland", Graceland. She experienced the glory and fulfillment of this marvel on two holiday visits, a year apart, while living with Irene. The initial "entrance" encompassed a two day visit right before Christmas in 2016. To say the least, it was an extraordinary phenomenon, to be greeted so warmly and highly by all of the great folks at Graceland and to be so graciously treated by everyone. The enchantment of encountering her father's beautiful grave on the site at Graceland was the most affecting and stirring involvement ever!

The emotional impact of driving up that infamous lane and arriving home for the first time after 56 years was amazing in itself! But, the wondrous surprise that was soon administered to her was way over the top of her dreams. She was asked to help decorate her dad's grave for Christmas with beautiful flowers and roses.

In a very important addition, Elaine had a spiritual happening with her father. It was raining, and she could not get her umbrella to stay up. She felt that her dad was saying, "Let the world see you on camera by my side." After praying at her father's side, she left before the visitors arrived, and in walking down to the gate, her umbrella opened up by itself, working perfectly again! Elaine smiled, looked up and said "Thank you, Dad!"

Before she came back to St. Louis, Elaine had the profound pleasure of going down to her dad's house in Mississippi and entertaining fans there, showing them around and swinging on the swing like she used to do as a kid in the UK. One of the fans said, "We know you are family because you look like Elvis sitting there."

The following excursion to Graceland happened in 2017 for a three day venture revolving around Christmas. It was another tremendously enjoyable and satisfying time! What made this trip very, very special was that she was put in contact with Elvis's best friend from early childhood. Leroy. It was a thrill beyond measure to go to his home in Arkansas and to meet him and his son, Michael. Of course, the memories abounded, and what a profound pleasure it was for Elaine to hear all of the great stories, not to mention the cheerfulness of seeing the classic original guitar that he and Elvis had bought together with every penny that they could jointly scratch up!!!

In between these two momentous and unforgettable visits, in July of 2017, Elaine was notified of this published announcement by Sherry Jane Cooke, AXS Contributing Writer (Part of AEG Entertainment):

"This gem (As Below) made more magnificent by the perfect step cut in this emerald cut diamond, making it look like endless stairs to the depths of perfection is the heart and soul of Elaine Elizabeth Presley , daughter of Elvis Presley while he was in the U.K. She is true, honest and finally accepted by the Presley family and estate! Elaine Presley has been a hero to me! She refused to give up her truthful birthright as a daughter of Elvis. I knew her before the results were in! I felt her connection with her father much and she is now an accepted and beloved member of the family. God accepts the truth and works to restore relationships. I love you, Elaine Elizabeth Presley."

Traveling to Sing

Two very stimulating out of town musical events were on their way to unfold…In August, 2017, Elaine and Irene were invited to attend the X-Poze-Ing Music Awards show at the Madison Street Theater in Chicago, and they were both honored with the request to perform. Elaine had already been declared the mascot of the ceremony, as the daughter of Elvis, and Irene was pleased to have previously won their Best Song awards in two categories. It was marvelously exhilarating for both Elaine and Irene to receive accolades at the end of the show. What a celebration! Elaine was bestowed with the "Outstanding Musician" award, and Irene garnered the two top awards of the year for both "Folk" and "Singer/Songwriter".

Elaine was very excited to represent her family in being a part of a big extravaganza for saving the animals of the world, "World Peace for Animals" at the Isis music hall in Ashville, North Carolina on November 19th, 2017. She got a huge bang out of being on stage for this event with famous hall of fame artists and bands. When she gave her spiel, she proclaimed to the audience, "Don't be cruel…to the animals!!!...and then she launched into singing "Don't Be Cruel".

The Utmost Gifts

Elaine and Irene were astounded and overtaken with gratification when they were notified in 2017 that they each were having customized painted guitars made for them by the renowned artist and minister, Austin Turner in Memphis. This was indeed a high honor! They were informed that Turner always considers these works of art, not gifts from him, but gifts from God. Indeed, this was such a magnificent tribute to Elaine from her family, and for Irene's sake, this was the family's way of saying "Thank You for writing the special book about Elaine's life".

Elaine and Irene were so ecstatic upon receiving their guitars that they took videos of each other opening up these gems! Step by step, hand by hand, until the treasures burst out of the box!! Amazing… Each one so perfectly crafted not only in artistry, but in personalized execution, designed with the rich identity of the owner and portraying individualized theme through style, color and natural character.

And, unbelievably, not long after, Elaine and Irene learned that they were also about to receive an "icing on the cake", as if they had not already been bestowed with the iciest icing on the biggest cake already!!!

Austin Turner was in the process of creating his highly regarded "Austibirds" for Elaine and Irene. These exquisite birds were gloriously handcrafted in fine detail with each proud recipient in mind. Oh, what another jubilant reception was about to unfold!

Each "Bird" could not have been more gorgeous and deliciously completed! It was a fulfilling effort to hang each one of these treasures on the wall in Irene's living room.

Synchronicity Abounds

Call it serendipity, synchronicity or simply fate, but there was a whole surreal lot of it, uncannily and meaningfully happening to Elaine and Irene ever since they first met!!! One wild correlation after another! And it just seemed to get bigger and deeper all along! Whether it presented itself as little stuff or big stuff, each realization and/or occurrence was poignant and brought it all together!

There are so many instances and situations to document, , but here are some highlights, both on the light side and the profound side, that are worth noting. (In each case, it became penetrating to both Elaine and Irene that there was a strong spiritual factor that was being played and planned out from above, on the part of both Elaine's dad and Irene's dad! And, these mystifying bits were in addition to the numerous numerological sequences that are brought forth in another chapter!)

- Irene's childhood sweetheart, true love and forever friend, Gene was from Memphis, and he spoke with great pride about his knowing Elvis and playing baseball with him.

- In April, 2011, Irene had the thrill of being cast in the movie, "Teenage Atomic Zombies in the 21st Century" as co-star with Everett Dean, the Rockabilly King, who was a popular local rock artist known for his dramatic entertainment of Elvis songs. (In the film, he played the Prom King, and Irene played his Prom Queen.)

- Elaine and Irene, in summer, 2016, went to the exciting musical performance of "All Shook Up" at the famous St. Louis Municipal Opera. It was a revival of Elvis's greatest hits incorporated into a zany and captivating plot. There were so many unbelievable moments in the production which chimed in alignment with Elaine's life that her goose bumps were bursting!... One was the name of the amusement park in the small fictional town where big scenes were played on one of the main stage sets. The name was featured on a huge backdrop sign, and it was "Funland". That strikingly caught Elaine's eyes, as it was the same as the amusement park in Great Yarmouth in England where Elaine, as thirteen year old David, had worked during the summer.

- Also, quite eerily, a pertinent and pivotal part of the plot involved the girl star who fell madly in love with the star playing Elvis' counterpart. She was rejected by him, and so she dreamed up a method by turning herself into a boy, thus becoming close buddies with Elvis and in clever, creative strategy, eventually winning him over...In her pretending to be another person and a boy, and showing keen sensitivity as a loyal and caring friend, she/he was able to touch a penetrating note with "Elvis" and catch his attention and affection in a way that he would not have noticed otherwise. This whole scenario totally bowled Elaine over and over! Even though the circumstances were completely different, it rang a real bell regarding Elaine's life history. It was not only the transitional aspect of the girl/boy, boy/girl issue, but mainly the whole reality that was so powerful in Elaine's early life as David, in naturally owning the female essence of being able to feel, understand and empathize in a way that typical boys don't have a grasp of and which made the girls comfortably gravitate to him. (This was that same strong element that came to mind in watching this segment in the production. The natural female component of the actress was "coming through" to "Elvis", hidden inside the guy image, and that was what made the difference.)

- All of this was on top of the weird actuality that Elaine and Irene had parked the car, of all places amongst the many spots in lots and along the road in surrounding Forest Park, right behind a car bearing the license plate, reading in forefront, MA 6…The day of Elaine's huge revelation. (May 6, 2013.)

- Elaine received two phone calls in early 2017 within the same week from two people who did not know each other, who were helping Elaine. They said that Elvis had just come to them to thank them in a dream for helping Elaine.

- Irene's second husband, Chris' grandmother became friends with Elvis. He remembered, as a kid, when his family would travel from St. Louis to Memphis annually for many years to visit Elvis at Graceland. Interestingly, his grandmother had a striking resemblance to Elvis' mom, Gladys, and on occasion, she was mistaken for her. (Irene got a kick out of commenting: "My former husband, Chris' grandmother looks a lot like Elvis' mom, Gladys!

And, my great friend, Elaine's grandmother also looks a lot like Elvis' mom…because she is!!!")

- Elaine was immensely joyous upon meeting Chris's mom, Bobbi (Irene's former mother-in-law), whom Irene invited to come over for a visit and to meet Elaine in early 2017. It was an extremely touching afternoon visit which lasted eight hours! Elaine was mesmerized with all of the Elvis memorabilia that Bobbi brought with her, from letters, postcards and 45 records, to pictures with Elvis from visits to Graceland to a personalized, Elvis signed movie still in a frame…

- But, the winning, tear jerking, highly emotional moment was when Bobbi presented Elaine with a darling small vintage frame holding the original dried roses from Elvis's grave that her mom had brought home with her after going down to the funeral. (Bobbi had saved these treasured rose petals and had herewith placed them in this customized frame for Elaine.) Elaine was especially and overly taken by this lovely surprise, as two weeks prior, Elaine was praying to her dad in asking for a small momento from him.

- The meeting between Elaine and Bobbi was beyond special, and Irene was elated that Elaine was so overjoyed! It meant so very much to Irene to watch and hear her dear friend, Elaine and her ex-mother-in-law, Bobbi building a bond. It was at a time when Elaine was feeling the brunt of the "Haters" and disbelievers all around. But Bobbi, who had already established a good spiritual bonding with Irene, connected with Elaine and sincerely kept saying, "I believe you." (In sadness, Bobbi only lived another few months. And, how eternally grateful Elaine was to have gotten to know her, even for a brief but such a meaningful time. And how equally thankful Irene was to have captured those wonderful moments in time!)

- Irene's little yorkie is, of course, named Grace! And, of course, the big dog at the neighbor's house across the street is named Elvis.

- Irene lives in the suburb of Brentwood in St. Louis, Missouri. Elaine went to boarding school in the town of Brentwood in England. Plus, the Presley family, including Elaine and daughter, Bridgette lived or have lived in Brentwood, California.

- In March 2017, Elaine and Irene had the supreme joy of attending the truly magnificent musical performance of "Million Dollar Quartet" at the St. Louis Repertory Theater. Of course, Elvis was one of the main characters, and to put it mildly, this show brought the house down from the ceiling, down and up again, a million times over!!!!! There were so many synchronistic vibes during the show that effectively carried away Elaine and Irene…too many to convey but heavily making an impact and "bringing it all home"!!!

- On April 9, 2017, Elaine was overwhelmingly grateful to Irene for taking her to the celebratory funeral, a four and a half hour service at the Pageant in St. Louis, honoring the life of the legendary original King of Rock and Roll, Chuck Berry. There were so many amazing testimonials, especially including one by a famous singer who talked about a vivid memory of when Elvis walked into an establishment where Berry was performing and pointed out to him on stage, "That is the real King of Rock and Roll!" (Elaine especially wanted to go to this important event for and on behalf of her father and the family. It was an occasion that her father, spiritually through Elaine, would not want to miss, in celebrating the life of the original king of rock and roll.)

- Around this time when Elaine was having really hard emotional nostalgia, one early morning she came down stairs to be confronted with a perfect image of Elvis's face illuminated in Irene's family room window. It manifested from the break lights of Irene's car, which malfunctioned and turned on, creating a bright 3d effect of the image within the entire family room. Elaine knew it was her dad, and she was mesmerized, with a feeling of protection and peace from her father. Till this day, the image of Elvis remains in Irene's back window.

- Irene was so excited to introduce Elaine to Victoria Price, the daughter of Vincent Price! It all happened when Victoria came to St. Louis in March, 2018 to give a talk and book signing regarding her new book, "The Way of Being Lost". What an overwhelming jubilation it was for Elaine, the daughter of the King of Rock and Roll to meet the daughter of the King of Horror!!! The two King's daughters had a blast, to say the very least! (Irene's mother, Dorothy had a long romance with Vincent culminating in their engagement in 1935. Dorothy had to break the engagement due to family matters, but they stayed close friends until their deaths, only 16 days apart, in 1993.) Elaine wholeheartedly expressed to Victoria, "It's so very special to meet you, as I feel close to you and your father through living with Irene. I have said since I came to live with Irene that I was saved by the King of Horror for the King of Rock 'n Roll!" And, Victoria was overly elated to meet Elaine and insisted on having photos taken of the two of them.

- During Victoria's talk, she spoke often about her history of feeling "lost", which of course, rang a humongous bell with Elaine in her being "lost" for so long, just as Victoria, yet in totally different ways. What struck a big note with Irene were the inferences that Victoria shared about her finding her truest self by letting go of all of the pressures put upon her that she should do this and do that...and instead, just tuning into her heart and being herself! That was exactly what Elaine was doing too, and it was also exactly what Irene was living her life doing. When Victoria summed it up with the importance of feeling "Joy" every single day, that almost knocked Irene out of her chair, as that joyful theme had been a thankful focus for Irene for a long time and was especially now playing an impactful role in Irene's life!

- The other compelling perspective that Victoria spoke about was the "meaning of life", which she conveyed, as part of the above, and which Elaine and Irene had constantly communicated about and continually discovered, more and more, in finding the real answers.

- As Elaine and Irene were driving home after this moving and inspiring discussion, Elaine broke into the verbal exhilaration of how she tremendously felt that this recent experience was a "meant to be" and bringing her to full circle of being part of the Price/Leland family.

- One of the biggest changes in Elaine's life was when she was exclusively invited to attend the Elvis Presley "The Searcher" documentary private premiere with Priscilla Presley, the woman Elaine considers to be her mother. After all, it made sense because Elvis Presley is her father, who is eternally in love with Priscilla. And Elaine had an unexplainable motherly connection. This highly earmarked early movie showing and cocktail reception was held at the Belcourt Theater and Cabana's in the heart of Nashville, Tennessee on March 18th, 2018.

- The documentary unveiled many key and driving actualities, and in its unexampled way subtly endorsed the life of Elaine. Elaine was not surprised that she felt even more close to Priscilla seeing her in person. It was almost like Elvis was reaching out in spirit to bring everyone together. The film itself was as if it was also telling the story of Elaine as well as of Elvis. From the bike scene in the beginning with the playing cards and pegs in the wheels to the fascinating "roadmap", searching for who they both were (meaning Elaine and Elvis), leading to the conclusions and enlightenment.

- Both Elvis and Elaine always managed to stay calm on stage even though they could feel terrified before going out to perform. There was a spiritual presence behind this because they both had the ability to read the individual audience members and to be able to deliver a finely tuned response naturally.

- Factually, Elvis and Elaine, unbeknownst to each other, visited black churches, and there has been a lot of incorrect information about why they did this. The truth is that white churches did not give them the musical, soulful feel that they needed. Black people did not teach Elvis or Elaine how to move their legs and hips. This was already natural for them to do. Black churches gave them both the spiritual vehicle that they needed to bring out and release their deep, soulful feelings that they both had inside of them.

- Elvis became lost after the death of his mother. Elaine became lost after the death of her father. Elvis found himself intensely searching all of his life, trying to find the answer to the purpose of his existence. When his career took him down many dark roads, he became even more lost. But, by going through this painful process, he found that what he was searching for was already inside his own heart...and that is Family, which is the real Foundation, of course...God, and thus Happiness. In his seeking journey, he created a natural "road map", which he passed on to his family.

Elvis's destiny was to entertain his fans, and that is what he did to the highest degree! The roadmap Elvis naturally created was a mighty gift for Elaine and Lisa and a privilege, something that Elvis was not fortunate to have for himself.

- Elaine also received another great gift on the day of the documentary viewing, and it was a gift from Priscilla Presley…Priscilla's inspirational words of creating projects and meaningful missions opened up Elaine's eyes…that she was now feeling really "Home".

- Irene was overjoyed in September, 2018 to have one of her original songs, "As You Dream Tonight" signed, recorded and produced in Las Vegas by the infamous Clarence Collins, Founder of Little Anthony and the Imperials and distinguished member of the Rock and Roll Hall of Fame. During the excitement of meeting Clarence, she mentioned her upcoming biography about the life of Elaine Presley. Clarence chimed in right away stating that he had enjoyed a longtime friendship with Elvis! He and his wife had spent many years "hanging out" with Elvis and Priscilla!

- In the summers of 2019 and 2020, respectively, in Nashville, Irene was thrilled to record her two songs, "Cracks in the Sidewalk" and "Wishing Well", after having them selected for label and production by the well known award winning record producer and former Grammy board member, Doc Holiday. Excitingly, she was so moved to hear from Doc that he had been a very, very close friend of Elvis! Doc was also really good buddies with Elvis' bodyguard.

The Big Deal

About four years after Elaine "came home", she was approached by a confidant and associate of her father to create an offer for her to hand to the executives of Authentic Brands, which purchased the rights to Elvis Presley. The offer comprised of five million in cash and approximately twenty million in rights, assets and privileges. But there was only one catch. The confidant wanted to change Elaine's voice on any recordings and the way that she represented herself as a person.

Since Elaine had been lost and had no confidence before she came home to her family...and then became totally found on May 6, 2013, there was no way and no amount of money in the world that would ever get her to change who she is!.. No way! It was natural.

So, Elaine declined the offer, stating that she wanted to stay being herself.

This made the confidant upset, since he had spent weeks on trying to re-train Elaine into the way that he desired her to be. But he got over it, and the confidant and Elaine remain friends until this day.

Later Elaine realized that some of the things that the confidant wanted to do made sense to her survival within a big corporate world, and now Elaine remains herself but follows rules set for her in order to have a life at home within her family. The powers to be control everything, in the same way that they did with Elvis. Elaine so far has been able to remain being herself, and at a very costly monitorial price!

Just like her father, she is kept in a box where people want her to be. Elaine always remains herself, just as Elvis remained himself, in a controlled world, where they have to do what is required and not always what they dream.

This is summed up in one of Elaine's father's quotes: "The image is one thing, and the human being is another." This lesson is part of the roadmap that Elvis Presley left his family: To maintain "being yourself". And within that, "to be great!". And "to never allow anybody to change you into a false persona that you cannot continue to live up to!"

DNA Exposed

When Elaine first realized who she truly was and shouted it to the world, the world reacted with, "Okay, show us your DNA test, and then we will believe you!" But it was not as easy as that, because when she did take her DNA test, the world responded with, "No, no, no…it's fake DNA!" And, it did not help either that Elvis's body guards were still trying to protect him, in saying that anybody claiming to have his DNA was false. In all honesty and in anybody's rational mind, how would any of these security people even know? It is only hearsay. And, then there are executives, fans and media trying to protect her dad as well. And, Elaine really does appreciate all of these people, and she too, believes that most of the claims seeking money are indeed fake. However, this protection really hurts a real child trying to go home.

We all know that the media does not make money off of positive stories. And, if Elaine had been fake, investigative reporters would have had a field day by now, and Elaine has been investigated by a lot of them. It needs to be remembered that Elaine has given up her life to come home to her family at Graceland, in continuing her legacy. It upsets her that the outside claimants have no real desire to "come home" and continue their supposed father's legacy. Elaine Presley herself has stopped millions of dollars in faked claims, in protecting her father's legacy and pocketbook.

However, when you are the real child of Elvis Presley, it is extremely painful and frustrating when you have to fight every inch of your way to be home at Graceland, desperately wanting to continue your legacy and to build Graceland, in using your God gifted and learned skills, yet in all that time, being held back by ignorant people who fail to correctly see who she really is. Elaine did not "come home" to gain money. She has a tremendous amount of business skills, many of which Graceland has already taken advantage of. She would be a success without being a kid of Elvis Presley. The only reason she came home was because Graceland is her home, and she is devotedly fighting to be able to do her job that is within her rightful legacy. But, how does a real, legitimate child of Elvis Presley, when the world surrounding him is filled with so much ridiculousness and insanity, do her dutiful job???

Well, the first answer is to solve this question of DNA. In Elaine's defense, she has been completely honest, open and transparent since the day she realized who she was. Additionally, this book is a complete and accurate document of her entire life. Now, as Elaine clearly conveys to anyone out there, "You can totally know me really well. There has never been anything hidden. There are no excuses. And, there are no reasons why I cannot show you something. This book is the whole truth and nothing but the truth, so help me God!"

So, let's get down to the cold, hard DNA investigative facts. In herself, having experience as an investigator, she will now display the facts of investigating herself. Her very first investigation was by the British government. And, no one ever said that she was not who she was. Her second investigation was by Homeland Security and the FBI. And, it needs to be explained that this was an extreme investigation, including intense interrogation and inspection of her entire life, including blood tests, finger prints and a mental/physical examination. In results of this extensive four year criterion, she was evaluated and confirmed to be Elaine Presley, daughter of Elvis Presley and her paperwork shows this.

Even though the government has Elaine's father listed as Elvis Presley and recognizes her as such, the federal government cannot endorse "out of Wedlock" children. It is the United States federal law.

The next investigation was done by a private security company in France. In taking her DNA from finger prints, they kept most of the testing secret, yet they sent her a quick message saying that she definitely was the child of Elvis Presley.

The next validating evidence came from the media. They executed an examination of her daughter, Bridgette and her sister, Lisa Marie. Through facial recognition and the latest ear DNA technology, which has been proven to be 99.6 percent accuracy, the media lady came back to her and stated that, not only are they related, but in their resemblance, they looked almost like twins. Elaine proceeded to ask her if she could publish this finding. The reporter said that if she were to do that, being that Elaine's family was so powerful, her career would be over. This further explains why no media has ever published that Elaine is fake. In addition to this, they have also never published any elaborate story in the press either because the simple truth is that this is no elaborate story. This is just the simple truth.

Now, so far, just nonbelievers can still say that this is all rubbish. And, Elaine herself, even with full government approval, has not seen her complete DNA results. And, she needed to see them! She needed them on file. She needed the results to be in a form that could never be altered, so that no one could say that they had been tampered with. She also needed family to have access to the results. Thus, she set off on a mission to accomplish this for "you", anyone out there! This became a very important mission for Elaine, as she understood that many people in the public may need absolute evidence that "You are you", and that's all there is to it!

Ultimate Evidence

We need to start out with the fact that Elaine was born in the UK. And, as far as anyone knew, her mother was English, and her father was also English. English heritage goes way back, and they were 100% English, unlike in America, where there is a big mix of lineage. Many English people have pure breeding. Her adoptive parents were an army and farm family. They served in the 1st and 2nd world wars and still do serve in the armed forces till this day, serving England in the army. They travel to and from places like Germany and Iraq. They are a strong family of army heroes. If her dad had been her real father, she would have been proud to follow in the family footsteps. But there was undoubtedly something that was kept out of the picture regarding Elaine's life, and for such a long and tormenting time, she did not know what it was. Elaine cannot put into words how lost she felt. It was truly horrendous.

Thus, as noted, she is supposed to be one hundred percent English. And, this would mean that considering her DNA, all of her relatives would be in England. There would be no way that she would have any element of America or any other country in her DNA. But, the father that she claims to be her rightful father is in big part English and European. Many people who were born in America who have English ascendants can obviously have a very high percentage of English DNA. Elaine's DNA, firstly, rules out the dad with whom she grew up.

Her DNA positively shows that Dennis Charles Mower was not Elaine's real blood father. In fact, there is no trace whatsoever to his heritage in Elaine's DNA.

Herewith, we are going to explore who Elaine's natural father is, in true knowledge of her assertion that it is Elvis. Her DNA tests show that Elaine is: English, Scottish, Welsh, Irish, European, (German, French etc.) American, Cherokee and Melungeon. She has all of the markers in her DNA, and the same Y' DNA that her father, Elvis has. And, even though she was born in England during the army's activities, many of her relatives show up as being in America with the same mix of DNA spread throughout the world, with her first 3 cousins related to the Smith and or Adkins family, from Tennessee.

When a DNA test is run, a surname is not used. Rather, they take one's raw DNA and enter it into international data bases. That then starts the ball rolling in attaching surnames based on DNA evidence. If the first father, Mower had been her real father, then he and other names connected to Mower would show up. But in Elaine's case, overwhelmingly it showed up as Smith, Presley, Wallace, White, and all of the other related family surnames stretching through time. Elaine's DNA heavily places her in Virginia, North Carolina, Mississippi and Tennessee. Of course, there was still the evidence of English and European heritage stretching through European countries out to India and into West Africa. It is the western European heritage and connection to the Adkins family that makes the Presley's to be

Melungeon, and it is the White family, southeastern rare B DNA heritage that makes them Cherokee.

Elvis Presley's DNA was run a couple of times when he was living, and later, in the course of time, it became confusing to know whether that DNA was real or fake, as some of the findings had become tainted. However, Elvis's original Y DNA, according to Haplogroup evidence published online by historians and Elaine's DNA are a match and contain a rare B gene. It is undeniable that Elaine's DNA is on both sides of Elvis Presley's family, making Elaine and Elvis related. Taking in all of this clear evidence and considering the fact that Elaine Presley is so much like her dad in so many ways and the certainty that her DNA places her smack in the middle of both sides of the Presley family, as previously explained, as well as Mississippi and Tennessee through DNA, and relatives DNA, it is pretty genuine and unmistakable about who she is.

With the new DNA technology today, anyone can see who they are in doing a fair amount of research, locating relatives and locations. It's not a mystery anymore... just simply hard DNA facts.

But, just in case there are still any doubters, the public needs to know that Elaine's DNA was analyzed by the world's top DNA scientists, placed in the world's largest and most advanced DNA matching system, and stored in The University of Arizona's medical research university.

Elaine's final DNA narrows her down to settling in Tennessee with the possibility of just two hundred fathers. And, since Elaine's DNA markers and Y DNA match Elvis Presley, plus with all of the other evidence combined, Elvis is her father…in a factor of billions to one. DNA of her father came from very reliable official sources, connecting both sides of the family's DNA.

Here are Elaine Elizabeth Presley's DNA facts:

Within DNA, there are two ways to determine paternity. The first and most common occur when the father and child are still living. The DNA samples of both parties are sent to the lab, and the lab sends a letter back showing the paternity results. The second method, in the case when the father is deceased, is to take the child's DNA along with the father's relative's DNA, in putting together a DNA family tree.

Luckily for Elaine, DNA science historians have published Elvis Presley's DNA on the internet. And, all together, the DNA matches Elaine Elizabeth Presley, along with cousins who have available DNA, on both sides of the Smith and Presley families.

Furthermore, Elaine was born in the UK. But part of her DNA places her in Tennessee with some of her closest cousins; including X match cousins who are also from Tennessee. In fact, out of 1707 matches of Elaine, they all connect, either way, on both sides of the Smith and Presley families.

Elaine's Birth Certificate

Details of Elaine's birth certificate are as follows:

David Mower does not exist. And, the reason for that is that all of the records for David Mower have been sealed or deleted by the American and British governments. And, this was executed due to a court order based on decisions made by the court, changing all of her legal and medical records in both the UK and United Stated, to Elaine Elizabeth Presley.

Her birth certificate reflects that she is a girl, Elaine Elizabeth, born in Clacton On the Sea, Essex, England.

In 2018, a further order was placed, based on 2017 DNA evidence that Dennis Mower is not the biological father of Elaine Elizabeth Presley, formerly David Mower. This action removes him and adds the correct parental information, as it is known to be Elvis Aaron Presley.

A Child of a Legend's Reality

In Elaine's words:

"One would think, as millions do think, that in being related to a legend, that one's life is simply and completely filled with an entitled and privileged existence with unlimited money and endless partying. And, in a way, it is true. I am awarded more than most people do receive. And, people out there look up to me and admire me for who I am. And my job in exchange, is to act accordingly to family and society rules in order to continue my legacy correctly for the public. This is a huge responsibility, and it is interesting that my original thoughts were to be a regular person in regular clothes supporting people.

I later realized that because people look up to me, the public does not want to see me hanging around out there trying to be like everyone else, because I am not like everyone else. They want to see the full blown branding of who I am within my legacy. I was trying to give the public my respect by trying to maintain my down to earth self. But, it does not work. I am out there in the world, as part of my legacy, and people surprise me all of the time with wanting hugs, photographs, autographs etc. I am not an ordinary person. I am part of a legacy, and I have to live up to my role within my family. There could be a tremendous downfall and massive backlash for me if I could not do just that and live up!

Being who I am really hit home to me when I thought that I could go out and apply for a job to earn extra income, in order to build my career faster. And, I was hard hit with my circumstances. Being who I am with my fame can create problems for companies who are interested in hiring me. A simple job interview can become more like a celebrity 'meet and greet'. Organizations that are not used to hiring celebrities can become overwhelmed in that I even applied. In addition to this, I am not just representing the company. I am also maintaining the image of my family legacy. And, whether I am working for an organization or attending a hit Broadway show, my presence could be taken as an endorsement. And these examples, as such, have to be correctly licensed and paid for, which comes under our legacy management for image and branding.

So, as you can see, I cannot just do anything I want to, because everything has its rewards and consequences. Everything has to be by contract and approved because I am in and representing our family. At this point, my responsibilities hit me hard. I then immediately, upon recognizing this reality, upgraded my attitude and my image to the high level that the public along with my legacy demands of me. And, from that place, I continue my legacy. I've gotten my act together, and I focus just on my family, my company, my foundation and my career within Graceland. I have been smacked in the face and smacked into shape!

And, you may be thinking: How can you possibly do that? Isn't it impossible to go from trying to live a normal life to all of this big stuff?

And, my answer is simple and direct. No, that's my job. That's what I do. That is my role and my position…to live up to our legacy and to continue it. And, this should give you an insight of what celebrities have to deal with on a daily basis. We do things that are hard. We make things happen from nothing, and we create. On the other hand, being me is not all that simple. Many times, I have to go out and I have to cope with being recognized and always acting in accordance with protection of our legacy, along with treating the public with the utmost respect. I have to represent my role within my legacy continuously at the highest level, 24/7, 365 days a year. It does not matter if I am tired or not, I still have to live up to my role.

In addition to all of this, there is the subject of money. Since I am in a famous family, it seems like everybody is scheming to get my money. Then one must understand that we are controlled by rules, companies, managers, advisors, etc. And, most importantly, at the time of this book's publication, I do not receive a large allowance from my upbringing. I, as a famous kid, am subject to amazing pressure. And, being freshly home in my family, I have to learn how to negotiate as far as what I want. Nobody just hands me a load of money. I quickly found out that I am dealing with a powerful bunch of management executives that I may have to potentially sue and/or make deals with that are good for me. If I make a bad deal, these execs would have me pinned to the wall. It's not a 'lovey dovey' situation. It is a ruthless and emotionless business environment.

When I first arrived home with who I am, with a big smile and wanting to love the world, come to find out, in the first four years, I was slaughtered! I am responsible for being strong and making my own accurate business decisions. Being a celebrity child, I am not always wanted. I can be seen as a risk, threat or asset to the management team. Nobody is going to hold my hand. I have to stand on my own two feet with the gifted talent that God and my father bestowed on me, and thereby make a successful life for myself, within my family."

The Heart of the Matter

Unquestionably, there are many types of genders. In this important segment, Elaine wants to inform and elaborate on this subject, so that the reader can better understand the truth and facts and myths behind gender identity disorder, GID, also known as Gender Dysphoria.

Most people think that there are two genders, male and female. And, this would actually be correct. However, it is not all black and white. There is a big grey area where things can get mixed up at birth. We have all seen men who are very effeminate, and we have seen women who are very manly. Now, both of these "grey area" people have the correct brain for their individual sex. The effeminate man is actually a man with a man brain. And, the butch woman is actually a woman with a female brain. There are essentially no issues or problems with them because they have no desire to change. They are "grey area" people who are content with who they are. The challenge arises when you tip the balance and place a female brain in the male or a male brain in a woman. This marks the entrance into the world of the transgender.

And, until recently, there really was no science to verify and understand these "mixups". The system of knowledge is much more clear now as to knowing whether one is supposed to be a girl or a boy, regardless of what genitals one may have been born with. There are advanced developments that can pinpoint exactly what kind of brain a child has, so that ultimately that uniquely different kid does not have to grow up dealing with and struggling with gender issues all of his or her life. In having the correct brain for the correct body, a person has harmony. Everything in the body must be aligned. The mind must work together with the heart and soul, the body makeup and the gender. It all works in unison. And, if one of these aspects is "off", it can have devastating consequences.

Medical technology also has the ability now to understand how and why some sexual parts are mixed as both male and female. This offers a unique opportunity for parents with children who have gender dysphoria to keep a watch over them in eliminating the misfortune of these offspring growing up and having to hide their feelings and true selves…in a gender in which that they do not feel comfortable. Therefore, the hopeful goal would be to set in motion a way to fix the situation at an early age of possibly somewhere between five and ten.

In fact, this was within the age bracket that Elaine, then David was when the doctors first deciphered that he/she needed some form of corrective surgery. At that time, the science did not exist to determine the correct sex. The questions used in trying to determine the right gender were along the lines of "Do you want to play football?", etc. And, even though David hated football, he was told to say that he liked it. And, this sadly resulted in his spending many months in the hospital to make him more of a complete boy. And, dismally no one understood this realization that he had the female makeup in his brain, except for his mom and grandma!

In recognition of fairness to the doctor, David could see on his face that he was unsure if he was making the right decision for him. The doctor, in respect to also being fair, then told David that he could wait until later on to make up his mind about the proper choice. But, the doc informed him that by not having this corrective surgery at that time, there could be a higher risk of getting cancer, being that David's body had elements of both genders.

David, himself was scared of this "false" father, Dennis that was with him. And he was embarrassed to tell Dennis that he wanted to be a girl, since Dennis was a hardened army hero and a farmer/logger. He had improperly pressured David to tell the doctor that he loved playing football and boy games, with the intention of later getting rid of David by making him enlist in the army. So, David did what he was told. On top of that unbearable constraint, David was never given a proper explanation of what kind of operation he was going to receive. All he knew was that he felt like a girl and he was too scared to talk about it.

In Elaine's later giving the physician more credit, she strongly states that the doctor seemed to have a natural understanding more about these complex gender issues at a time when the science was not there. As she rightfully puts it, there are some people who may think that God made two genders, and that anything in between was evil. This is what some preachers, especially those of the "old school" would like to tell you. And, this is so far from the truth:

David had been going to church on his own since early childhood and loved God. Elaine knows that God made us all the way we are for His own good reason, and that He loves us all. Herewith, Elaine wholeheartedly expresses her feelings to you, any reader out there who suffers from any kind of gender disorder: "Do not, for one second, listen or buy into anyone that says that God hates you because of your gender dysphoria. This is simply not true!"

As you can see, Elaine's gender issues occurred at birth. And, what is compelling is that if that doctor had made her female in that early surgery, then no one would be saying anything. But, because she had to suffer for many years in different genders, it opened the doors to a lot of controversy. Yet, the plain facts are that Elaine was really a female all along. Due to lack of science and a controlling stepfather, she was made to be male on the outside. Henceforth, after many years living inside the wrong gender, she was able, with the help of the new department of learning, to finally live and to be who she really was as a woman.

Accurately, Elaine did not suffer from any kind of mental problems, apart from the fact that she had to painfully handle being in the wrong gender for such an extensive time. Nonetheless, after the final correction of this quandary, she now lives a regular and fulfilling life as a female. Elaine as herself is not transgendered. And, this is backed up by thorough medical examinations by doctors and psychiatrists. In fact, the very last words that the physician said to her on completion of her transition, "This file is closed, and there is no reason for you to come back. So, get out there, live your life and be happy!"

Elaine relives so vividly her recollection after that last appointment, as she was skipping down the street, feeling very elated and happy and saying to herself, "Well, that's it, I'm done!" There is no doubt that

Elaine is and always was a female who had former medical issues. She is one of the lucky ones and has been able to undergo a completely normal life as a girl.

The only challenge that Elaine had with men who wanted to date her was that, in the beginning, as she was quite sexy, they would mistake her for some sort of sex machine. The reason for this was that Elaine was going through her teenage years again as a new girl dressed in little mini skirts and tops. And, she had to vigorously let these pursuers know that she did not necessarily enjoy the prospect of being swung upside down by chains, while blindfolded and being whipped by leather whips. She was a normal lady who enjoyed normal sex, which sometimes might include subtle sex couple antics, such as a light spanking every so often while possibly being dressed up in black fishnet stockings and purple panties, but only if she was with the man of her dreams, not with some "psycho", sexually deranged pervert!!! All of Elaine's sexual desires were within a normal range, not the extreme.

Quite obviously, Elaine has not had one iota of interest in the guys who are only thinking of fettish, kinky "one night stands"! But, wait a minute! In her pondering over the puzzlement of all of this, "Why do guys think like this in regards to girls like Elaine?" It was probably due to her form of attire, placing her in the world of slutty, wild gals on the lookout for adventure! (This does not imply that all girls who dress up in a sexy manner are seeking sex.)

As far as dating, this is where Elaine wishes to speak about her first dating experiences. This is in relations to her pre-op (before surgery) and post-op (after surgery) procedures. Elaine was still in her first two years of corrective transition. She was going to gender meetings and settling in to her normal life as a girl while waiting to have her corrective operation. In this time period, men wanted to date her. Elaine did not attract gay men at all. And, the straight guys who wanted to date her were kindly told by her that they needed to wait as she had not yet had her corrective surgery. Nevertheless, these men still wanted to take her out on dates, buy her roses and give her a kiss. Elaine was always treated as a regular girl, right from the beginning.

Destiny Revealed in Numerology

Ever since the birth of David who truly was and became Elaine, she has always been very spiritual within herself even though the family did not go to church. As a child, "she" went to church on her own. She has relied heavily on God throughout her life. She has seen angels. She has been told that she has a spiritual soul. She shines as a light so bright, and gypsies and spiritual leaders have told her that she has been connected to Elvis Presley in a previous life, this life and future lives.

Even though Elaine did not know understandably and officially that she was the daughter of Elvis until later on, she has been connected through destiny her entire life to Elvis Presley. She may not have realized that he was her father until 2013, but her soul had known it and has been connected to him all of her life. People may think that she never knew her father, but she has known him very well since the very beginning. And, her great inner sense of "synergy" and "connectiveness" has pulled Elaine Presley towards her father... until that one remarkable day on May 6th in 2013 when she found her "way home". And on that day, all the stars aligned, and Elaine Presley was found in mind, body and soul.

It is a very real and powerful phenomenon that Elvis Presley himself from heaven brought Elaine Presley home as he had promised her as a child. But can this destiny of the Presley family be seen and tracked? Or is it just an unseen spiritual connection that the family shares together? There is strong evidence in the world relating to and revolving around the spiritual mystery of Elvis Presley.

Both Elvis Presley and Elaine Presley were deeply involved in finding the truth about the meaning of life through God, spiritual sources and numerology. And, it is definitely through numerology and DNA that the lives of these two individuals can be traced. Not only does Elaine Presley look so much like her father and have the same traits, but they have lived extremely similar lives doing similar things.

In high regards to numerology, their roads and patterns in life can be "footprinted". And, this aspect brings new testimony to the world that in regarding the question, "Is destiny random or is it set?", Elaine believes that we are all part of a big universal plan.

The number 24, that was always important to Elvis and also to Elaine, yields an ideal metaphysical vibration. It all starts here:

Elvis Presley was drafted into the army on March 24, 1958.

Elaine Elizabeth Presley was born in 1959. 1+9+5+9 = 24.

Mildred Hynard was part of an army family, and she lived a half mile from the Colchester army barracks, which transported soldiers to and from Germany. She moved from Colchester to Coggeshall on 42 Tey Road. (42 reversed is 24.)

She raised David, now Elaine, at this address, and David moved to London in 1977. 1+9+7+7 = 24.

Elaine then moved to America at age 24.

Elaine's daughter, Bridgette was born when Elaine was 24.

Lisa Marie Presley was born in 1968. 1+9+6+8 = 24.

"2001: A Space Odyssey". Beginning in 1971, Elvis used this theme to open all of his concerts. Elvis studied the numerology book, "Cheiro's Book of Numbers". He passed away on August 16, 1977. 8+16 = 24.

1977...1 + 9 + 7 + 7= 24.

At the time of Elvis's death, he was 42. The number 42 in reverse is 24.

24 + 1977 = 2001.

1935 + 42 +8 +16 = 2001.

8 + 16 + 1977 = 2001.

David "passed away" at age 42. At the same time, Elaine Elizabeth Presley's journey in diagnosis to become herself began at age 42, when she was "born again". (42 in reverse is 24.)

Elvis Presley's comeback was in 1968. 1 + 9 + 6 + 8 = 24.

Elvis' mother, Gladys was born on 4/25/1912. 4 + 2 + 5 + 1 + 9 +1 + 2 = 24.

Gladys and Vernon were married on June 17, 1933. 1 + 7 +1 + 9 + 3 + 3 = 24.

The headstone in the 1957 movie, "Loving You" reads "1878". 1 + 8 + 7 + 8 = 24.

Elvis Presley's role model was James Dean. James Dean died at age 24.

If this is not enough to convince you about the meaning of numerology in the Presley family, then keep on reading!!!...

Elaine Elizabeth Presley returned to singing in 2011. She started to realize who she really was in 2012.

Elaine met Irene online on 6/6/'12. 6 + 6 + 12 = 24.

In that year, people were predicting that the world would end in 2012. What they did not realize is that it did end in 2012, but not in the way they thought. It ended, and a new spiritual world began. This allowed people to connect and communicate much more easily with each other, whether dead or alive. If one remembers, people were predicting in 2012 that Elvis would return on his "death day", August 16th. Everyone was feeling imminently that the actual return of Elvis Presley, as they knew him, was about to happen.

Elvis did not return physically. Yet, people felt his spiritual return. So, these steadfast fans felt that this event would ultimately still happen on the same day in 2013. And, thousands of people congregated at

Graceland to celebrate and welcome him for his return. Again, Elvis did not "show up".

Truly, in the same year, three months earlier, what was happening was that Elaine was receiving the declaration of revelation from Elvis that she was his daughter, a forthcoming promise that Elvis had given her at the age of 13. He had told her that one day in the future she would need him and that he would be there…And, in the meantime, that she must live her life as normally as possible.

This greatly caused Elaine to feel anxious for many years… What was going to happen, and how did he know what was going to happen? This forced Elaine to live a very straight life and to stay as healthy as possible, including no drugs and no smoking. Elaine realized fully who her daddy was at that surreal moment on that extraordinarily memorable day of May 6th, 2013. And, she also had a strong and secure sense that he, her daddy, was very much in the spiritual mode of taking the best care of her.

From that second on, Elaine had instant confidence in the knowledge of knowing exactly who she and her family were. Backed up with the memories of the past and the fact she was so much like him all of her life…along with multiple other evidences, she knew that her father had just "brought her home" and that she was the kid of Elvis Presley. And, this moment with her father was a "homecoming", a real life miracle that she will never forget…as she went from being totally lost with no confidence to being totally found …something that she will never forget.

Previously, before the age of 42, Elaine was Elvis' son, David. Elaine, in newly "being home' and with a world of Elvis fans thinking that Elvis was about to return again, this frightened Elaine because all these people were waiting for Elvis to come back. And, Elaine had just "come home" at the same time that all this was happening.

In retraction, many Elvis fans did not believe that Elaine was the true offspring of Elvis himself, and she received hate and death threats beyond any scope of imagination. As part of Elaine's determined and unrelenting efforts in dealing with this harassment and emotional invasion, she set her mind to zero in on an important conception:

Elvis and Elaine Presley loved the snow, and in 2015, Elaine told her fan base that it would snow within two weeks, based on the fact that she was praying to God and to her father to make it snow as in the old days! The simple fact was that there had not been a heavy snow in Memphis for a long time! Along these lines, people everywhere, including in Memphis, laughed at Elaine Presley, in telling her that it does not snow in Memphis!

Yet, within those two weeks, it snowed in Memphis harder than it had ever snowed before! Folks all over the place were emailing and calling Elaine Presley saying it was "blizzarding" in Memphis! And, even Elaine Presley's home at Graceland made a video of it! And, this, Ladies and Gentlemen, is how Elvis and Elaine Presley returned "home" on May 6, 2013 to Graceland.

And, 5 + 6 + 13 = 24.

When Elaine accepted the supreme invitation to her father's private preview of the Elvis Presley documentary, "The Searcher", she was extremely honored to be there along side of Priscilla. The route that Elaine traveled to arrive there was US 24.

Priscilla's birthday is May 24th.

Elaine was at the Priscilla Presley Distinguished Citizen Award Dinner in Memphis Tennessee on June 24th 2018.

In huge conclusion, the 2001 Space Odyssey is being replayed in cinemas on August 24, 2018.

And, the original final version of this book, "Kid of the King" (now, "The King's Kid") was completed on August 24, 2018.

The original copyright registration date for this book was dated 7/6/2018. 7+6+2+8 =24. (The copyright was made official in November, 2018.)

The latest edition of "The King's Kid" was finalized on March 24, 2022.

Enter Elvis

All throughout Elaine's ascending life, the Elvis factor, in pure essence of true reality and supreme spirit was always there… surrounding her, watching over her, guiding her and saving her. Regardless of the fact that for so many years, this truth of Elvis Presley being her father was hidden and "hushed up", Elaine subconsciously "knew" all along, and her soul would take her on an evolving and culminating path.

Overall and comprehensively, in regarding the facts about Elvis and his kid, many exact details remain hidden, and whether or not she, born as David was conceived in Germany or England.

Elaine feels in her heart that Elvis would today be with Priscilla or at least be best friends with her. He loved all the women he dated, but they were "bandages" hiding from his true love, Priscilla.

No doubt, as already relayed, the moving phone call from young teenager, David to Elvis speaks for itself in meaning and impact. Those poignant words from Elvis to his son say it all: "Just live your life and be happy. I will be there for you when you need me."

And then, of course, the remarkable illuminating reawakening for Elaine in 2013 when she had the strong spiritual connection with her father and realized that she was indeed Elvis' child.

The one thing the world needs to understand is that Elvis Presley continues to be here for Elaine to this day. And, this author has witnessed many unexplainable and powerful little "miracles" surrounding Elaine and her father. There is no question in Irene's mind that Elvis is Elaine's dad, and he lives within and around her.

It becomes more and more evident that Elvis left Elaine and Lisa a distinctive road map to follow, as guidance within their lives. Here is one out of hundreds of things Elaine has learned and continues to learn from her father:

"My father taught me, 'If you have fame and wealth without happiness, what do you have?'…And, I believe the same as my father. I like the level of fame that I have earned…just enough to live a life of happiness without the pressure. Health, Family, Self and Happiness are all we need. I am following our family road map."

In Reflection of My Daughter

As stated previously. Bridgette blossomed into being a very wholesome, mature and well rounded (not to mention, well grounded) young lady! She is very intelligent. She became a successful model. She graduated from college as a skin specialist. She also owned several successful businesses, a beauty care business, a legal services business and health products business. In Miami, Bridgette ran a top beauty and skin salon with luxury yacht services. She appeared as a main actress in "Miami Nights". She was a sophisticated host, and she now lives with her husband and two sons and a daughter.

"I was, needless to say, radiating over my daughter! In retrospect, the two of us went through a lot during the divorce of her mom and me, along with everything that transpired. Plus, we moved around quite a lot. We actually had a lot of fun mixed with sad times. (I feel that this is a common fact among many parents with offspring, dealing with this situation.)

There were many little times that Bridgette and I both remember, in the old days of selling signs. One in a particular and on a humorous note, was when we stopped off at a roadside café, and we both agreed on ordering the soft crab sandwich. When the order was brought to the car, we opened up the wrapping, and the sandwich had the crab in it, but the legs were hanging out! So, in holding our sandwiches in our shaky hands, we both looked at each other and started screaming and laughing! Then, in simultaneous stupor, we said, 'What the heck?' By daring each other, together, at the same time, we plopped the sandwiches into our wary mouths! In two little crunches and two big shrieks, the sandwiches went out the window as the foot went on the accelerator and the car went skidding out of the parking lot, but not without Bridgette and me bellowing out, 'That's disgusting!!!'…"

Elaine, as David, remembers well, telling Bridgette, after they drove down the street, that in light of this experience, "You better do well in school! Otherwise, you'll be going down the road, selling signs, like this, for the rest of your life!"

Another funny time that Elaine/David recalls with Bridgette was when they were in the food court of the mall in Virginia Beach. Bridgette was about five years old. David was having curried snacks, and Bridgette was eating chicken nuggets. He looked at her and said, "These are really hot!" She asked to try one. He said to her, "Okay, I'll give ya a bet. If you can eat one of these, I'll give ya five dollars." No sooner than that was said, Bridgette gulfed it down, and then she put her hand out and gave her dad, what is now known to be the "Presley look" and said, "Five dollar!!!" And, of course, David gave it to her!

Bridgette and her dad had a very close father/daughter relationship. They had so many wonderful fun times, full of excitement and education. Bridgette was very lucky because, even though her dad took care of many job situations, he was mainly self-employed, working only about two hours a day while his daughter was at school. She never ever really saw him work, other than in the early days, selling signs. He used to get up in the morning, fix breakfast, travel to school with Bridgette, give her lunch money…then pick her up and bring her home, cook her dinner, stay "on top of her" doing her homework and occasionally take her to movies or shopping in the mall.

They also used to watch movies at home, as well, and sit and talk and chat, laughing and playing games like Monopoly, cards, etc. They loved an old English card game named "Snap". He used to make sure that she got ready for bed on time. He read her made up bedtime stories that were often wild and crazy. Then, he kissed her on the cheek or forehead, saying "Goodnight, see you in the morning and love you!"

In order to help Bridgette sleep and to live a comfortable, happy life, David decorated her room however she wanted it. He surprised her with life-like stars and the moon on the ceiling with shooting stars. Thus, when he turned out the light, instead of being in darkness, her whole ceiling opened up into a midnight sky. And, she fell asleep within a few minutes. David's daughter pretty much had a nice life, with trips to Disney World, playing with friends, going to theme parks, shopping, going to movies and eating out with a solid, supportive home life.

On weekends, they used to travel to neighborhoods looking for their dream homes…that big white house with the lions and an electric gate. He never really found his dream home, but now he/she knows that the home he was searching for was his family home, located at, 3764 Elvis Presley Blvd., Memphis, TN 38116, USA: Home found on May 6th 2013.

At this time, again, it makes David realize why his father, Elvis Presley did not want him to sing and have a music career at a young age. He wanted him to live his life first and then "come home" later…and in Elaine's case, it was on May 6th, 2013.

In Reflection of My Mother

In Elaine's penetrating thoughts of reminiscence about her mom and in her own words:

"My mother's favorite song was 'Green Green Grass of Home'.

I have two distinct memories, in being a baby. (I later became concerned, as people said that one's memory doesn't go back that far. But, I remember it so well, and I knew it to be true. When I checked into this matter, I found out that you can indeed have vivid memory going back to early childhood, especially when there is a shocking impression.)

There are two main occasions, as a little child. The first is being at Nanna's house in the pram, by the piano in a room opposite from the living room. (This was in a very small cottage where my grandmother, Nanna lived.) I can hear them talking, (my mother and Nanna) minute by minute, laughing and having fun with the TV being on. I wanted to be in the other room with them, and I used to cry a lot.

And, I remember many other times, growing up being at Nanna's. We used to visit her quite often. She was very loving and caring, and so was my mother! You had to be careful coming in the front door, being slippery because of the rain. I remember it splashing on my Wellington boots. I remember just down from her cottage, there was a gate with an arching roof on top. I remember James and my climbing up the gate and inside the little roof. We used to play there a lot, and we wrote our initials in there. We used to walk the lanes and pick apples, pears and blackberries.

This is where I spent the most wonderful time of my childhood. Growing up, I remember being hyper and sensitive, quiet and shy and also noisy! Nanna used to sit with me and talk with me. She said 'Your dad played the piano, and you are a very special child. Your mum had a chance to be with another man, but she didn't do it, and I (Nanna) was upset with that decision. You need to remember always that you are from somebody very special.'

The other main occasion, in remembrance as a baby child, again in Elaine's words, is this highly treasured and emotional memory:

I remember meeting my real father when my mum took me to see him. He gave me a brown teddy bear with a moving head, arms and legs. I loved my teddy for my entire childhood. When I met this man, I was just a baby, but I remember him crying, like he wanted to take me, but my mum was very protective and became nervous and said she had to go.

This is the only time I ever met this man whom I now know to be my father, Elvis Presley. My mother was very loving and protective of me. I was her favorite. She looked after me very well and did everything she could do and more. Dennis, on the other hand, was vicious and violent verbally to me…One time, I remember getting into the car to go to Nanna's, and he looked at me in the car window and said, 'Get the hell out of here, you little bastard!'

Dennis made it clear that he was not my father, and he mentioned it a few times. I thought he was my dad, as I didn't know any differently."

.

In Reflection of My Marriage

Elaine's personal recollection and deep analysis regarding her former self, David and his relationship with Diane:

"From the time I met Diane, it was always a challenge because I suffered from gender problems and was very female within myself. I realize now that I had more of a female brain than a male brain, and Diane and I were more like sisters. Of course, we did all the usual things in bed, and she was a very beautiful woman. I felt she was happy with our sex life. However, I was never a 'guy/guy', and I sensed she was psychologically searching for that. And so now, after being a full female myself, I certainly understand that.

My focus was always on my wife and daughter. But I wasn't that full man that most women seek. I was more of a mother to Bridgette, and I still am to this day. I tried to be a man...really hard...but it wasn't natural for me...so unnatural, in fact, that also in being so pretty, my male friends did not like to go out with me because they felt feelings towards me. And, on separate occasions, a couple of guys both tried to kiss me. One of my friends, Bob actually told me that I should not go out with the guys that night as it was a 'guy/guy night'...really guy-like and tough!

I have come to realize that most male friends I had, being a man while married, were close relationships...more like a husband and wife than a guy to guy. And, as far as trouble in our marriage, in realization later,

I quite sadly believe that it was related to my gender issues. Romantic life was good, as I could feel what she wanted, but I just didn't have that manly feel that many women seek and that I also crave in men now.

So, there I was with my female brain, now fighting for custody of my daughter. Raising my daughter, Bridgette was the most beautiful experience of my life.

Diane and I ultimately filed for separation, and we agreed on joint custody of Bridgette. I had moved in with Max and his wife, Heidi in Virginia Beach, and Diane started 'floating' around from one place to another. When the divorce filing kicked in a year later, I filed for full custody…the reason I did this was that I wanted my daughter with me all of the time, and Diane was becoming more and more unstable in her poor dating choices. Later, of course, she too found the right partner, and has now been happily married for many years. We remain friends 'til this day!"

Additional Dramatic Developments

Herewith are significant, successive occurrences and fruitions:

After Elaine spoke with her confidant, she came to the realization that the custom home she grew up in that was built for her family may not have been given by the farmer. In real facts, farmers didn't build homes for laborers in England because poor families like David's were given English Council Housing with rent subsidies by the government. And, there was no one else at that time that was given a free house for working on a farm…and the home was totally free! And it is still in the family today, long after Dennis passed away.

In reference to the beginning of this life story when David thought that his home was given by the farmer, it becomes evident that it was more likely paid for by Elvis Presley.

On July 12, 2017, Elaine initiated her company, L and L Presley, an official Graceland Company owned by Elaine Elizabeth Presley and co-writers of the music " Graceland Anthem" by Elaine Elizabeth Presley and Lisa Marie Presley. Google verified. BMI Music.

Elaine was thrilled to be part of a great concert and cause held in Asheville, North Carolina on November 18, 2017. It was a cd release benefit for World Peace for Animals with Artimus Pyle. Featured on stage with the Lynyrd Skynyrd band were Lois Chazen, Elaine Elizabeth Presley, Natalie Jean, Arthur Strout, Jay Jourden, Artimus

Pyle, Christopher Chappell Pyle, Aditi Sethi, Jay Brown, Daniel Barber and Reggie Lafaye.

Elaine was blissful to be invited to attend the Priscilla Presley Distinguished Citizen Award Dinner at the Hilton in Memphis, which was held on June 24th, 2018. She relished watching Priscilla accept her award and also having dinner with her and guests afterwards!

It was comforting and rewarding for Elaine to receive this major letter of recognition on July 12, 2018 from the Commander of the Elvis Presley Memorial Post.

(See photo copy next page)

ELVIS PRESLEY MEMORIAL POST 11333

2600 ELVIS PRESLEY BOULEVARD

MEMPHIS, TENNESSE 38106

July 12, 2018

To whom it may concern:

By the power vested in me as Commander of the Elvis Presley Memorial Post
11333 Memphis I hereby appoint Ms. Elaine Elizabeth Presley to the Building
Committee of the Elvis Presley Memorial Post 11333 Memphis, Tennessee. Ms.
Presley is an integral part of the renovation and rejuvenation of our post. Without
her help our post would not have been able to maintain its beneficial presence in
this community.

Her father, Elvis Aaron Presley, was a veteran serving in the United States Army
Tank Corps in Germany. She is following in his foot steps as a proud supporter of
American military servicemen and women.

Sincerely,

Eugene Kelly McDuffie, Commander
Elvis Presley Memorial Post 11333 Memphis

Elaine is proud to have created and implemented her new "Princes and Princesses Children's Charitable Program". Here is the story behind it, in Elaine's words:

"It was one beautiful Christmas day in 2016 at Graceland. I had just finished having dinner with my friend, Julian of Capitol Records, when I heard this call from across the room at the Graceland Guest House Hotel. 'Hey, Elaine, come on over and talk to us!' I looked at Julian, and he looked at me. I smiled and said "Just go with the flow…""

It was a family from the UK, my fans. The first thing the gentleman, Jimmy said to me was, 'Are you okay, Elaine? How are you within yourself?' This was a lovely comment that moved me. I replied, 'I am doing fine. How are you?' They were all doing well too.

They insisted that I sing them a song. So, I sang, 'I Can't Stop Loving You', which was good because Julian later said that it was jaw dropping. He was so impressed that he gave me an open invitation at Capitol Records anytime. He even suggested that he would come down from California with his crew to record me in the Jungle Room…maybe on the following Christmas.

(This has not happened yet because my sister, Lisa Marie has been recording, and I do not want to step on my sister's toes.)

The following morning, I bumped into the same couple when they were getting ready to leave the guest house. I had time to get to know them a little bit better. Firstly, I could not get out of my mind the remark that Jimmy asked me about if I was alright, and I thanked him for caring so much.

It turned out to be a great fan photo opportunity, and I had the delight to meet their little girls. One was about two years old and had previously had some kind of brain surgery. I received permission to have her sit on my knee for which she had the biggest smile that lit up the room! Then it became time for me to make my exit. I never had the chance to do something that I regret to this day....to give that precious little girl a teddy bear.

This has played on my mind over the last two years, and it was the basis of my designing my latest charitable program for the Elaine Presley Foundation at Graceland, called 'Princes and Princesses Children's Charitable Program'. The program works like this: Every child from birth to nine years old who is unwell, living with a major illness, who visits Graceland from the start of this program on December 24, 2018, will be eligible with a valid Graceland ticket to receive an Elaine Presley Foundation teddy bear.

The application will be available at the beginning of this program at elaineelizabethpresley.com."

It is noteworthy here to bring recognition to the other creative additions that Elaine has contributed to Graceland. She states:

"One of the great benefits of 'being home' at Graceland is that I get to design things for my family, proudly assisting our entire team, in continuing our legacy. Even though my road home gave me many challenges, it was also the most wonderful journey.

My successes so far over the past five years have proven that I can stand up on my own two feet to represent Graceland. I have been grateful for several media credits, including radio, TV, stage, etc.

I am proud that I have been behind important causes: I am an advocate for anti-bullying, and my charity, 'Elaine Presley Foundation' assists adults, children and pets on a daily basis. I re-instated Rock N' Roll on June 15, 2013, by publishing a news release. I have attended major events for our family history, and I am thrilled that my sister and I have jointly created our Graceland Anthem, to be released soon.

In addition, I am pleased that I have contributed other designs, improvements and ideas for Graceland, of which some have been beneficially utilized. These include multi currency on the Graceland website, photos of Elvis fans, the Graceland vacation layaway program, a camp where children can come to start their music career, the Graceland rose garden, a kid's crafts and painting area and a Thomas Kinkade, known as the 'Painter of Light', master Graceland Christmas limited edition art to exhibit at Graceland.

I am happy to announce to you my latest concept for my Graceland team. My in depth research shows that within 300 miles of Graceland, and, I'm sure beyond, we have the type of Elvis fan, who has either visited Graceland before or has never done so, but desires to do so. The one amazing thing that I discovered is that the vast majority of these fans of all ages do not know about our latest improvements, the Guesthouse at Graceland and our new entertainment complex.

Here is my solution: To extend our tour buses into tour coaches, picking up and returning home. The tour coaches should have movies and historical videos all about Elvis. This plan could increase our visitors from 600,000 a year to over a million.

I am grateful that people within my fan base have either already visited Graceland or are planning to take on this adventure!"

On a very decisive level, Elaine was invited to come down to Memphis and conduct a very important board meeting at Graceland with eight board members of the VFW Memorial Post 11333. She spearheaded this two hour productive meeting on November 3rd, 2018, in the country board room from 3PM to 5PM.

The meeting was highly successful and assisted in forging the future of Whitehaven, the community surrounding Graceland. Elaine's role as part of her estate is to merge the Elvis Presley name into an existing memorial post by re-naming it the "Elvis Presley Memorial Post 11333". The original Elvis Presley Memorial Post was formed in 1954 and continued until 2016 when it eventually closed. The post was then re-located from an industrial part of town into Whitehaven. And there it sits now, reopened by Elaine Presley of the Presley Family estate, the Commander, Eugene Karen McDuffie and all of the board members.

The plan is to continue the legacy of the Elvis Presley Memorial Post, while assisting veterans and the residents of Whitehaven. But, as set forward by Elaine, it also importantly includes improving the neighborhood, and thus people's lives. This is indeed a moment in history, as Elaine Presley is now at home, not only following the roadmap that her father left her, but, in doing so, enhancing the whole district surrounding her family's home.

On January 7th, 2019, Elaine was jubilant to receive a stirring proclamation in recognition of herself and her father, Elvis. It was happily and respectfully sent from Philippe Piot-Umecker, a corporate security expert in France:

"Concern / Kid of the « KING « DNA Biography

By Philippe, Roger, Georges PIOT-UMECKER

It is well known that Elaine Elizabeth Presley, a native of Little Clacton on Sea in Essex, England, has brought unwavering love to her illustrious father Elvis Presley. It was not easy, it was not in the customs at that time to be able to recognize the direct relationship between a father and his daughter outside a line of conduct already drawn. But they were father and daughter and in unison, here is the beginning of a whole, the beginning of a life and a great love. A father, a daughter, Elvis & Elaine Elizabeth is a galaxy of music, songs, sweet looks, struggles in the life before and now, it's a force that can cross all borders. It is a perpetual vibration, it is the art of a myth and its legend working in the most indisputable reality.

I love history but not stories that are in my opinion perpetual disappointments and they do not stop making chimeras and utopias! The solidity of the true allows to annihilate the rumor !!!

Without this love between Elvis and Elaine, I do not think Elaine could have had this overflowing rage to excel in all her creations. And nowadays Elaine still holds the helm of the Graceland ship to continue to perpetuate the leading role of her illustrious father Elvis across multiple generations around the world. We can only applaud the professionalism, flawless motivation and integrity of Elaine's ongoing work to keep Elvis's melodies and songs alive ...

However, the fact remains that Elvis Presley has been able to be worthy of a true father by surrounding her with all his love. In short, is it not more important to have this recognition of love and protection from her father? Certainly, yes Love is always triumphant on the evil of the words of some and the perpetual skepticism.

I feel outraged sometimes when I can read or hear nonsense about the non-veracity of affiliation between Elaine Elizabeth Presley and Elvis Presley. I think that in human nature the contradiction, the rejection of evidences allow some to be valued in the eyes of the world and society. However, if a few decades ago the contradictory aspect could germinate, it is not questioned today thanks to the dizzying progress of high technology. Mostly the advances on DNA are to this day more than 99.9% indisputable.

The debate must be closed, and it is high time to get back together it is a matter of ethics, deep respect and love for ELVIS Presley but also for Elaine Elisabeth Presley giving all her life to continue to share with us each moment, each song, each musical note of the King 'Elvis'.

I am a privileged friend of Elaine Elizabeth Presley and as such I could have postcards, mail or even an old bank card. Of course, these effects are well kept because I consider them as the continuity of the work of her father ELVIS. One day I had the opportunity to read words denigrating the true affiliation between Elaine Elizabeth Presley and her father Elvis Presley. Wanting to silence these unconditional negative people I embarked on a DNA research proving the real existence and concordance between the DNA of Elvis and Elaine.

The results are eloquent and positive, so I do not understand this violence and this challenge when the obvious jumps out at us.

On the other hand, the debate can be opened on all the subjects like for example the works of Thomas Edison and Nikolas Tesla, on the works of Michelangelo because it employed 200 sculptors in his service. So which works are really of him?..of Leonardo da Vinci? Was the sculptor Auguste Rodin not overtaken by his pupil Camille Claudel? We could go far in these contradictions but that would lead to nothing, except to question the value and the works!

Of course we can, throughout our lives, compare, criticize, make absurd assumptions, but it remains an important point of view the power of love is creating positive waves between human people. Elaine

Elizabeth Presley is a bearer of hope, love, courage and a total involvement in what she best excels at writing, singing and playing roles to satisfy our daily lives and while perpetuating the memory and the works of Elvis Presley ....

Thanks again, Elaine Elizabeth Presley

Philippe, Roger, Georges PIOT-UMECKER, FRANCE."

Elaine was soon to be gratified to have Philippe become her special appointed advisor and consultant. This was all thanks, as she learned, to the connection between him and Priscilla Presley. (During the filming of the famous TV series, "Dallas", in which Priscilla had an ongoing role, she had become friends with Philippe's aunt, who was also in the cast of the production. Priscilla was honored to meet Philippe and impressed with his credentials. Philippe had a fine history of being protector/bodyguard/ sentinel for numerous figures and leaders, including the President of France.)

Philippe faithfully took on his new regular charge in advising Elaine and prepping her in all aspects of becoming her best, from her appearance to her conduct, regarding her important image and protocol as an integral part of the Presley family.

The ensuing maturation was about to take place. A pleasing and practical arrangement for Elaine and Philippe to be married! It seemed to have all of the elements of being perfect, in bringing the two together as not only a sound couple but allowing Elaine to have the fully automatic safety and support that she would undoubtedly need!

Plans started to unfold for a very luxurious and highly private "home" in a Beverly Hills high rise penthouse. Everything suddenly seemed to happen so quickly! Elaine was informed that Philippe's engagement ring was on its way, and sure enough, there it came! A gorgeous diamond!!! Elaine immediately treasured it, even though she was still dealing with the impact of all that had sharply transpired.

Culmination? Elaine decided to say "No" to the marriage. It was a painfully emotional, yet thoughtful consideration on her part. Yes, she had become entranced with the whole "setup" romance and opportunity. She found Philippe to be extremely attractive and strong! But, she felt down deep that there was something missing. She knew that she had to go with her "gut", on matter what!!! And, that is what she did!

Elaine was very pleased to release her very moving recording of "Scared Little Child", originally in 2019 and re-released under Liz Presley on May 5, 2021. In remembrance of her memorable experience as a child, here are her original lyrics:

"I went to the church 'cause I was lonely, feeling lost, feeling down, feeling scared. I prayed on my knees at the altar for God to guide me.

When I looked up with my eyes wide open, boy was I surprised…

Three angels were right there before me, so brightly alive.

God came to me to guide me, and I was just a scared little child.

It scared me, so I ran out of the church. I didn't get far before I stopped in my tracks… I slowly walked back to the church, with my heart beating fast in my chest.

The angels were gone, but I knew then that God had answered my prayers.

From that moment on, I felt not lost or lonely. I knew God was right by my side…no longer a scared little child…

No longer a scared little child…

No longer a scared little child…"

A momentous advancement evolved to confirmation in an unprecedented timely fashion in late 2020! After a complex legal process of seeking finalization of Elaine's renewed "green card", that could have taken a long time, she received the expedite news that she now has an approved and official permanent United States identification card! In astonishment and relief, Elaine ascertains that undoubtedly, her family was kindly behind this notable development!

In the midst of all the developments and happenings while living with Irene, Elaine kept thinking more and more about the possibility that Priscilla could be her mother, and she kept feeling a real and natural connection with her. There were also many significant signs along the way, from the times when Elaine was sent off to two important events involving Priscilla to Elaine receiving roses and card greetings from her "Loving family" on special occasions to the fact that Elaine was given special virtual vocal lessons twice a week by a prominent vocalist/instructor in Canada for almost two years to the advisorship of Philippe and the marital arrangement for the two of them.

Elaine was ever so grateful and fulfilled to be designated a main advisor and coach regarding her newly found family. It became clearly evident that this individual was highly regarded in his profession as an attorney and exclusively assigned as the confidant between Elaine and Priscilla. Elaine maintained (and still does) regular lengthy phone conversations with him, and she very much looks up to him and treasures his advice.

Certainly, a major factor of which Elaine has been made aware are the very complex and delicate circumstances considering Priscilla's juggling between her devotion to her family and the intense, confining rules in protecting its legacy.

(In keenly pondering on history, there seems to be a contradiction between the date set by the media when Priscilla met Elvis in Germany and the actual date allegedly established by family sources. The news still states that the two met at a party in Bad Nauheim in September of 1959. The assertion and true reasoning points to the meeting taking place months earlier in March. This importantly sheds light on the alleged and carefully hidden facts that Elaine, as David was born in December, 1959.)

In Elaine's continuing and arduous process of "investigating" and "fine tuning" the legitimacy of her proper birthright, as she vehemently was her own worst critic, she brought it all to confirmation on many levels and in many aspects:

- Elaine connects to her father, Elvis by multiple relatives and DNA tests, via private investigations for approval by Homeland Security and the FBI.

- She is the only other child approved of regarding her father being Elvis by Homeland Security.

- There are also over seven other DNA tests, all of which conclude that she is the daughter of Elvis.

- Plus, there is authorization by the "DNA Consultants" that she has her father's DNA.

- Private investigations in France passed her confirmation.

In tracing back through her heritage, Elaine found not only that Mildred Hynard was not her real mother, but that she was actually her cousin. Also, her "sister", Dora's son ran his DNA and discovered that he is a first cousin, once removed to a great, great uncle, fitting in with the Hood and Smith families on Elvis' side and relating Mildred with Minnie Mae Hood.

Elaine connects via DNA and family to Priscilla Presley, along the way of common ancestors. There is a long list which is readily available, of which the main antecedents are: Ramsey and Weiss.

Herewith on next page, please find the DNA main charts documenting Elaine's lineage to her father, Elvis and ostensibly to her mother, Priscilla.

(The chart regarding Priscilla matches relatives to X DNA for her within the range of 7CM and above to close family. The DNA relative's names are crossed out for privacy. The sheet matches four lines between Priscilla and Elaine.)

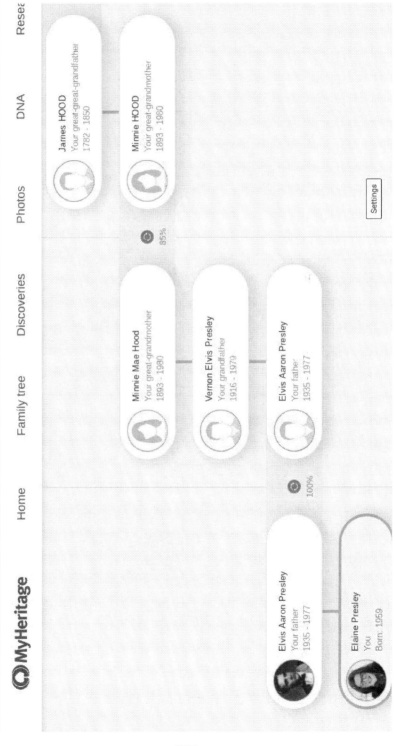

⊙MyHeritage   Home   Family tree   Discoveries   Photos   DNA   Rese

James HOOD
Your great-great-grandfather
1782 - 1850

Minnie HOOD
Your great-grandmother
1893 - 1960

85%

Minnie Mae Hood
Your great-grandmother
1893 - 1980

Vernon Elvis Presley
Your grandfather
1916 - 1979

Elvis Aaron Presley
Your father
1935 - 1977

100%

Elvis Aaron Presley
Your father
1935 - 1977

Elaine Presley
You
Born: 1959

Settings

327

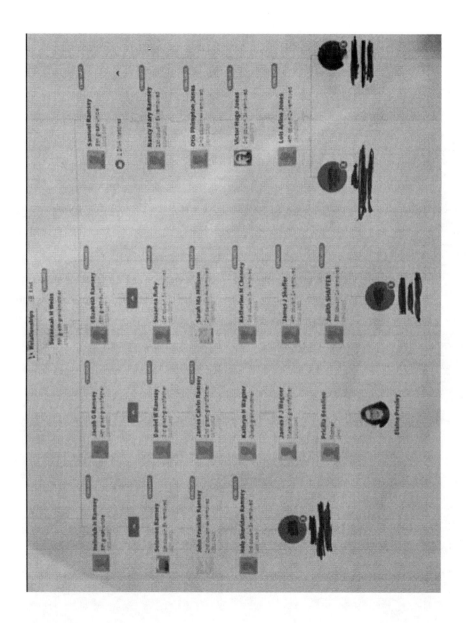

Also, here are Elaine's official certificates from DNA Consultants concerning her DNA ancestry to Cherokee and Native American:

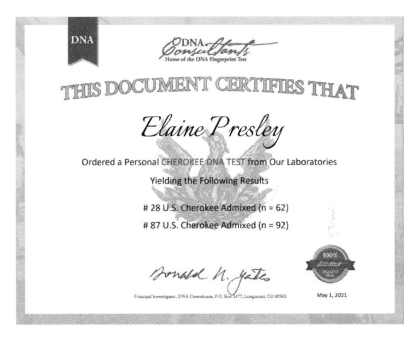

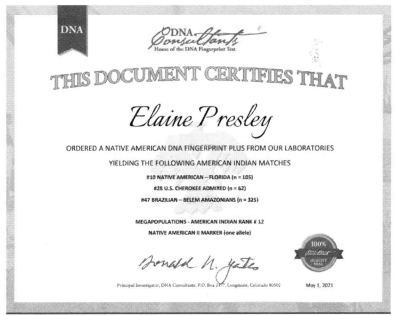

In December, 2020, Elaine found out about a remarkable, eye opening surprise that was waiting for her!! A gorgeous, huge, fully furnished mansion with sprawling land, tucked away in the beautiful woods on top of a little mountain in Tennessee!!!... And, to top it off, a luxurious Porsche convertible.

With many mixed emotions, Elaine and Irene bid a sad, yet celebratory farewell. Elaine headed on her way to her new home! What a sudden evolution and humongous advancement for her to take in! No time for goose bumps to even come into play! The lavish place was breathtaking, and Elaine could hardly wait to take Irene on a virtual tour!!! Such opulent and sumptuous surroundings! And yet, it seemed just right for her with a cozy, homey atmosphere. She says it is her dream home.

Elaine knew that this was a gracious gift from her family, and her gratitude was sky high!!! Talk about "déjà vu, come true"!!!...when Elaine used to look out Irene's front window, viewing the big houses and musing about what it would be like to live in one...Now, with each day unfolding, she realized that she was being given the best of care and protection by the family. She not only felt secure, but she was happy knowing that cousins on Elvis's side lived not too far away...

Despite her thankfulness for comfort and security, it didn't take long for Elaine to feel the constraints of strict guidelines and firm control. Was this the "being in the box" syndrome that Irene had talked about before and that Elaine thought was so enticing??? Oh, no! Oh, yes! Well, now Elaine was getting a first hand dose of what Irene meant when she felt squeezed out of her element and had to rebel! It all seemed to come together now for her as she vividly remembered Irene's memories. And, now here she was herself, living in a capsule of that big box which has the power to engulf you! But, no matter what the conditions or the forces that be, Elaine knew that everything was set up for her own good and that she was being well taken care of. She most assuredly felt that she was loved from afar…

Sweepingly, reality is reality, and Elaine has begun the adjustment of living in her new world as a celebrity child. In overall grateful measure, she is in awe and making the most of every moment, one venture after another!!!

I Am Me

Considering the big scheme of things, looking back and looking forward, in Elaine's expression:

"One of the amazing things that I experienced in being me is that people try to change me all of the time. They can see I'm like my father and through whatever reasons that they have, they think that being like Elvis is exclusive to Elvis. And it is. And we children, being like our father naturally, know it is not an act. It is who we are. I think maybe people get confused with tribute artists where people act to be like Elvis Presley. But we have to remember that that is an act, and simply that, and not who they are naturally. We, the family, are like our father naturally in his traits and mannerisms and looks. So, when people take a look at me, they do not want to believe that it is all real, so they try to advise me to change or to be different so they can feel comfortable within themselves, thinking that what they try to do to me shows that I'm no longer like my father. But I am me. And everything about me is real. Being like my dad is real. And I just want people to understand this…that I am me.

I should have realized who I was earlier, really, as I was just like Elvis Presley. But I did not realize it. And the painful truth is… when I became lost after my dad died in 1977, all the searching I was doing in trying to find myself…the sad reality is that I was already found and was running away from my dad's death. And, in all that I endured when and after he died, I was simply running from myself, trying to find myself, and my heart and soul were knockin' on my brain every second of the day, trying to tell me who I was. But my brain was on that fast moving train going in the opposite direction! And, I do know now that my 'lostness' was a combination of my hard childhood with Dennis, the man who I thought was my real father and the loss of my real father, whom I lost in 1977.

As a child, I was not allowed to have music lessons or sing. And to my amazement, it still is exactly the same today. I have been successful since I've 'been home', singing, doing 'meets and greets', recording and entertaining fans and doing media interviews. And all of it, except the things that are allowed, have been hidden, destroyed or taken away.

Back in 2014, when I did a show in Wales, England, the existence of that show was made to disappear. And, when I danced and moved my hips like my father, proudly, just like Dad, I was banned from moving my hips in public, with a hard, firm message. 'That's one nail in your coffin…don't add any more!'

So, as you can see, from childhood 'til now, I have been suppressed from singing, and I believe it is because I look and sound a lot like my father. Plus, after he died, it probably has something to do with the money too. Regardless of what the reason is, up until now, I have been made invisible to the public eye.

When I came home on May 6th, 2013, I thought the way I was doing things was right and loyal. I certainly now have learned a lot from my mother, as to protect my intellectual property, create at a higher level and run my part of being home like a business. And, I do today manage a small part of our estate.

I continue to work for our family/legacy and to release my best new creative works to the world, which I certainly hope people will enjoy!

This is my entire life up until now. Let's see what happens next...

I am me."

In Finality

This "King's Kid" has traveled a long way from looking over that bridge in Coggeshall, Essex, England when she projected that she belonged somewhere else. And, from that point, in searching and searching, on many roads along the way with many trials and tribulations, it was a long, long journey until that one day that a promise from her father finally came true! On May 6th, 2013, Elvis Presley brought home his other child, Elaine Elizabeth Presley.

And now, five years onward from that, Elaine had to fight, tooth and nail, to seal and claim her place at home...in Graceland. And she has done so with remarkable vision by not only retaining her place but building a successful debt free foundation and company through it all. Elaine is not only a prosperous business lady at home, but she has proven to be a major asset to a legacy, by already designing many things which move Graceland ahead into the future and with many more ideas to come.

This is not just a kid coming home to live within her family... Elaine is dedicated to the ongoing prospect of Graceland. So, hand in hand, with her sister, Lisa Marie and her mother, Priscilla and all of the children and grandchildren, Elaine continues her life 'at home" in Graceland, on behalf of her father, Elvis, in heaven with God.

"This book is the truth, the whole truth and nothing but the truth, so help me, God!"

THE END